Serving the City:

The Dublin City Managers
and Town Clerks

1230-2006

Serving
the City

The Dublin City Managers
and Town Clerks
1230-2006

Dublin City Public Libraries and Archive

Dublin City
Baile Átha Cliath

Published by Dublin City Council
Produced by Dublin City Public Libraries and Archive
138-144 Pearse Street, Dublin 2, Ireland

© Dublin City Council, 1996, 2006

1st edition researched and written by
Mary Clark and Gráinne Doran, 1996

Additional material 2nd edition written by
Mary Clark and Hugh Fitzpatrick, 2006

Manuscript photography by Alastair Smeaton

ISBN: 0946841 85 3

Typesetting, design and origination by
Environmental Publications, 5 Grafton Street, Dublin 2, Ireland

Table of Contents

List of Illustrations

Acknowledgements

Dublin City Council wishes to express sincere thanks to the relatives and descendants of former town clerks and Dublin city managers, who have generously contributed family information and photographs which are contained in this book, including: Sir Gordon Beveridge [town clerk John Beveridge]; Mrs. Elizabeth Byrne and Mr. Dominic Murphy [town clerk John J. Murphy]; Mr. Edward Stewart Gray [town clerk George Archer]; Mr. Max Keane [city manager John P. Keane]; James and Fidelma Macken [city manager Mathew Macken]; Mrs. Marie Molloy [city manager James Molloy]; Mr. Conor O'Mahony [city manager Timothy C. O'Mahony]; Mrs. Anna White [town clerks Thomas and Henry Gonne]. We are also grateful to Mrs. Brigid Clesham, who kindly allowed us to draw on her research into the Gonne family; to Inspector John Duffy, former archivist to An Garda Siochana, for information on Thomas Feely; and to Dr. Raymond Refaussé, for access to books and documents in the Representative Church Body Library. Barbara Dawson, director of Dublin City Gallery: The Hugh Lane, kindly gave permission for the portrait of Gerald J. Sherlock to be reproduced. Photographs of modern Dublin were provided by City Arts Officer Jack Gilligan, Divisional Librarian, Alastair Smeaton and by Paul Heffernan of Dublin City Council's Press Office, while dates of service for Dublin City Managers were checked by Ann McGrath.

This second edition of *Serving the City* incorporates text from the first edition, which was researched and written by Dublin City Archivist Dr. Mary Clark and by Gráinne Doran, now Wexford County Archivist. Additional text for the second edition was supplied by Hugh Fitzpatrick, City Manager's Department. Manuscript photography is by Alastair Smeaton, Divisional Librarian, Dublin City Libraries. The publisher on behalf of Dublin City Council is Deirdre Ellis-King, Dublin City Librarian.

Foreword
by
the Lord Mayor of Dublin
Councillor Vincent Jackson

The office of town clerk and the mayoralty of Dublin have a long and close historic connection. In February 1230, the first Mayor of Dublin, Richard Multon, presided at a council meeting which conferred land on the first town clerk, William FitzRobert. Seven hundred years later, in October 1930, the first Lord Mayor for the Greater Dublin area, Alfie Byrne, congratulated the first Dublin City Manager and Town Clerk, Gerald J. Sherlock, on his appointment to this new post. Since then, the Lord Mayor and the City Council have worked closely with successive City Managers to develop and enhance this great city of Dublin. The renewed sense of pride which Dubliners now take in their world-class city is proof of our success to date.

As Dublin City Manager from 1996 to 2006, John Fitzgerald has been pivotal to the modernisation and re-development of Dublin over the past ten years. As the last in a long line of Town Clerks of Dublin, in continuation from 1230 to 2001, and as the first Dublin City Manager of the new millennium, he has built on the best from the city's past while positioning it strategically for the future. On behalf of Dublin City Council and on behalf of the people of Dublin, I wish him well as he retires from his current office to take up a new position.

The Mansion House
July 2006

Glossary of Terms Used

Civic franchise:
Also known as the *freedom of the city*, possession of the franchise in the period up to 1841 gave the holder the right to vote in elections to the Dublin City Assembly. The franchise could be acquired by *service*, on completion of an apprenticeship in one of the Dublin trade guilds; by *birth*, as the son or daughter of a freeman; by *marriage* to the daughter of a freeman; by *grace especial*, reserved for people who were not members of a guild or who came from outside Dublin; or under the 1662 *Act of Parliament* for encouraging Protestant strangers to settle in Ireland. New freemen had to pay an entrance fee, known as a *fine*.

Clerk of the city; Clerk of the Tholsel; Town Clerk of Dublin:
These terms are used at different periods, and sometimes interchangably, for what is essentially the same office. *Clerk of the city* (or *clericus civitatis*) was favoured in the medieval period, when documents were written in Latin. *Clerk of the Tholsel* gained favour in the 16th century and was used until the middle of the 18th (although often replaced by town clerk). *Town Clerk* was used until 1930, when the then holder of the office, Gerald J. Sherlock, was promoted to the new post of Dublin City Manager and Town Clerk. For ease of reference, in this book the office-holder is called town clerk throughout the period 1230-1930.

Currency, Irish and Sterling:
Under an act of parliament passed in 1460, a distinctive Irish currency was created, with coinage called *Irelands*, *groats* and *Patricks* (later called pounds, shillings and pence). In 1552, Henry VIII decreed that the Irish currency was to be reduced to parity with that of England and the terminology was standardized. Irish coinage was re-valued in 1689 at a rate of £100 sterling to £108 Irish, but fluctuations were common. The two currencies were amalgamated in 1825.

Dublin City Assembly:
This was the civic government of Dublin until 1841 and consisted of the Lord Mayor, two Sheriffs, twenty-four aldermen, forty-eight sheriffs' peers and ninety-six elected members, representing the trade guilds of Dublin.

Dublin City Council:
Under the Municipal Corporations Reform (Ireland) Act of 1840, the Dublin City Council replaced the City Assembly as the civic government of Dublin. The City Council was originally elected by all ratepayers with a valuation exceeding £10 (*see below*) and it is now elected by all residents of Dublin City who are aged 18 years or over.

Dublin Corporation:
Dublin Corporation was the local municipal authority for the city of Dublin from 1548 until January 2002, with responsibility for civic administration. The Corporation performed a variety of functions assigned by the legislature to local authorities generally. Chief amongst these functions were housing, road transportation and safety, water supply and sewerage, development planning and control, environmental protection and recreation and amenity. Under the Local Government Act 2001, which came into effect on 31 December 2001, Dublin Corporation was abolished, and was replaced by Dublin City Council, encompassing the elected representatives and the civic administration in one organization.

DCLA:
Dublin City Library & Archive. This was established in July 2003 and consists of the Dublin & Irish Local Studies Collections (including the library of Sir John T. Gilbert) and the Dublin City Archives. The City Archives includes manuscripts, rolls and records generated by the Town Clerks of Dublin from the early 13th century onwards.

Rates, payment of:
Rates was a form of local taxation levied on all owners of property. The *rateable valuation* of the property was assessed according to its size and the *rate* of local tax was struck each year by the local council. If the rateable valuation of the property was £10 and a rate of £1 was struck by the council, then the owner of the property was obliged to pay £10 as a local tax for that year. In Ireland, rates on domestic property were abolished in 1977, but were retained for business premises.

Introduction

The city of Dublin has had a tradition of professional administration since the early 13th century, in the person of the town clerk. In 1930, the town clerk took on the functions of the newly-created post of Dublin City Manager and forged a new partnership with the elected Dublin City Council to govern and manage Ireland's capital city. This book seeks to provide an introduction to this process by examining the history of the office and looking at the personalities of those who held the post, first of town clerk, and later of Dublin City Manager. It is hoped that others may be drawn to this topic, where more detailed research still needs to be carried out, and the resources of the Dublin City Library and Archive will be available for this purpose.

The process of administration creates records and with the passage of time, these become historic documents which are described as archives. The work of the town clerk's office down through the centuries has created documentation which now forms part of the Dublin City Archives. Today the City Manager's Department, together with other council departments, continues to generate records which will become part of the City Archives in thirty years' time, as provided under the Local Government Acts of 1994 and 2001.

On 31 December 2001, the office of town clerk of Dublin was abolished, ending a tradition which had lasted nearly 772 years, and the last holder of the title, John Fitzgerald, continued as Dublin City Manager until his retirement in June 2006. As Dublin enters the third millennium, now as a world-class city, this affords a vantage point to look back over its long history of civic administration, while saluting the achievements of John Fitzgerald as City Manager.

Deirdre Ellis-King
Mary Clark
Alastair Smeaton

July 2006

The Town Clerks of Dublin, 1230-1930

Winetavern Street, Dublin. The year is 1230 and the citizens of Dublin have gathered for a meeting in the Guildhall. By unanimous decision, a deed is drawn up and a plot of ground at the New Gate is granted to William FitzRobert, town clerk of Dublin, "for his good and faithful service" in return for a yearly rent of one pound of pepper. The deed is witnessed by many of Dublin's leading citizens, including the city's first Mayor, Richard Multon. With due solemnity, the city seal is attached to the deed, which is handed over to the town clerk, to allow him to take possession of his new property.

In a society where few people could read or write, it is not surprising that the people of Dublin valued their town clerk so highly. The word clerk is derived from the Latin *clericus* which was applied originally to all men in holy orders, including bishops and priests. By the early 13th century, *clericus* had acquired a more specialized meaning and was reserved for men in minor orders (such as acolytes) who were not ordained and could not, therefore, celebrate the Mass, while the Latin word, *sacerdos*, was used for priests. In a further distinction, although bishops and priests were forbidden to marry, clerks in minor orders could do so. In 1230 (the very year that William FitzRobert received his grant of land from the people of Dublin), Pope Gregory IX decreed that every priest should be assisted by a parish clerk who would sing during services, read the epistle and lesson and be able to teach in the parish school. This pre-supposed a high standard of learning by the clerk: he should be able to read (in Latin), sing (in Gregorian chant) and write.

Viking Dublin had specialized in the production of tools and weapons, but was known for its oral rather than its written tradition. This changed when Dublin was captured in 1170 by the Normans under Strongbow. The Normans had built up a considerable empire through their superiority in war, but newly-conquered lands were consolidated by their efficient system of administration, which was made effective by recording all decisions in written documents. In November 1171, Henry II arrived from England to bring Dublin under the control of the Crown, and he then issued a royal charter granting colonization rights in the city to the men of Bristol, who had financed his visit to Ireland. A large influx of settlers resulted from this charter, with people coming mainly from the Norman dominions in Britain and on the Continent. Between 1190 and 1250, some 8,400 people were registered with the guild merchant of Dublin and these included some seventy men who gave their profession, in Latin, as *clericus*. Some of these clerks came to Dublin from Norman settlements elsewhere in Ireland, including Athy, Co. Kildare; Balrothery, Co. Dublin; Carrickfergus, Co. Antrim; Cloncurry, Co. Kildare; Mullingar, Co. Westmeath; Selsker, Co. Wexford; the town of Wicklow; and

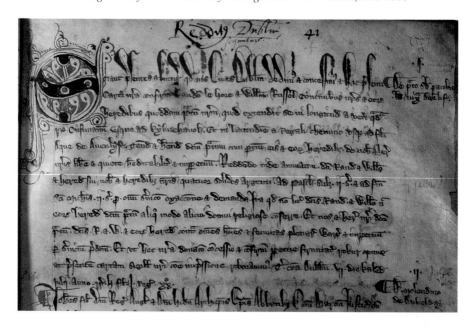

the cities of Cork and Galway. Other clerks came from Bristol, Carlisle, Chester, Coventry, Derby, Northampton, Winchester and Wingham in England; Cardiff, Cardigan and Haverfordwest in Wales; Greenock, Renfrew and Stirling in Scotland; and Arras, Nantes and Rouen in France. In the early 13th century, Dublin boasted twenty parish churches, so it is not surprising that clerks were drawn to the city in such large numbers, hoping for employment. But men with such high qualifications were also sought outside the church. Jordan, who registered as a clerk with the guild merchant of Dublin, later became an officer of the guild and was working in that capacity before 1222, while other clerks, such as Ernisius (who came originally from Newcastle-on-Tyne) were employed to witness, and probably to write, deeds issued by barons who held land in the vicinity of Dublin. It was in this context that the civic government of Dublin decided to appoint a town clerk to look after the administration of its affairs.

The office of town clerk may have been established shortly after the city was granted a charter by John, Lord of Ireland, in 1192. This defined the boundaries of Dublin and gave the citizens certain privileges, including the right to take possession of all lands and vacant places within the city's boundaries, to build on these and to set the lands out to tenants. Although surviving documentation from this period is scanty, we know that the citizens were issuing leases of common property before 1199 and the services of a clerk would

Grant of land at New Gate to town clerk William FitzRobert, 1230. (DCLA, White Book of Dublin, fol. 41a)

16

have been required to write out the necessary deeds. William FitzRobert was established as town clerk before he was granted the New Gate lands in 1230 but he may well have had at least one predecessor who was active after 1192.

In addition to the usual training of a clerk in reading, writing and Latin, FitzRobert had a further qualification: he had some legal credentials, and is described in contemporary documents as *William-de-la-Choife*. A coif was a close-fitting cap which was worn only by sergeants-at-law and, in an age where clothing indicated status, FitzRobert would not have worn any such garment unless he was entitled to do so. His legal training must have been invaluable to the city. In 1229, Dublin concluded complex negotiations with the Crown, and obtained a charter allowing the citizens to elect their own Mayor, thus securing a measure of independence and self-government for the city. The charter was issued by Henry III in return for releasing him from a debt of £312 borrowed by the Crown from twelve Dublin citizens. This debt was taken over by the city and was discharged by a levy on all the inhabitants of Dublin – and it was only then that the charter could be put into effect. The debt had been repaid by February 1230, when the citizens assembled for their first council meeting, to elect the first Mayor of Dublin, Richard Multon and, as we have seen, to grant land at the New Gate to William

FitzRobert "for his good and faithful service" as town clerk of Dublin. This "faithful service" probably refers to FitzRobert's role in negotiations for the mayoral charter and it is significant that one of the witnesses to this grant was Robert the Money-changer, who is likely to have facilitated repayment of the loan.

FitzRobert was town clerk for over thirty years and his main duty was the preparation of legal documents, which he wrote in Latin on parchment, using inks made of vegetable dyes and pens made of goose quills. Parchment was made from the skin of a goat, sheep or deer, and was supplied by Alan the Parchment-maker, who had registered with the guild merchant of Dublin in 1222. FitzRobert was also responsible for keeping lists of free citizens, that is

Roll of Free Citizens of Dublin, 1234-1249. Entries attributed to William FitzRobert, first Town Clerk. (DCLA, Fr/Roll/1)

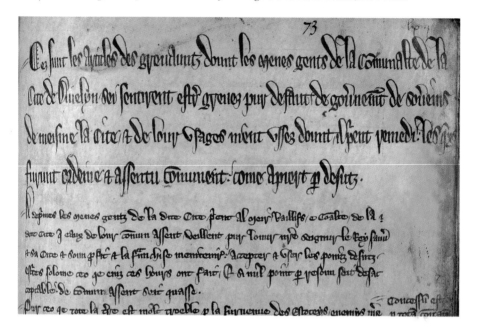

people who were entitled to vote in civic elections. A roll of free citizens has survived for the period 1234 to 1249 and is preserved in the Dublin City Archives. The names are written mainly in one hand, and although it is not signed, it may be assumed to be the work of William FitzRobert.

Grievances of the Common Folk of Dublin, c. 1315. (DCLA, White Book of Dublin, fol. 73a)

As a scribe, FitzRobert's work was plain and unadorned, but his successors in the 14th century began to illuminate their texts in a more elaborate manner. In 1311, the municipal government moved from the Guildhall in Winetavern Street to a new headquarters, the Tholsel in Bothe Street (later called Skinners' Row). This move seems to have prompted a re-organization of the city's records which were copied into two bound manuscripts: the *Liber Albus*, or White Book of Dublin, so-called because of the colour of its fine vellum, and the Chain Book of Dublin, which acquired its name because it was kept on public display in the Tholsel, chained to a lectern. Five years later, Edward Bruce, brother of the more famous Robert, marched on Dublin, as part of his campaign to establish himself as king of Ireland. To keep the Scottish army at bay, the Dubliners set fire to the western suburbs of the city and demolished the Dominican priory of St. Saviour's on the north bank of the Liffey, using its stones to build a new defensive wall along Merchants' Quay and Wood Quay. These desperate measures succeeded: fearful of a long siege which might prove fruitless, Edward Bruce withdrew from Dublin. In the chaos which accompanied the Bruce Invasion, ordinary Dubliners banded

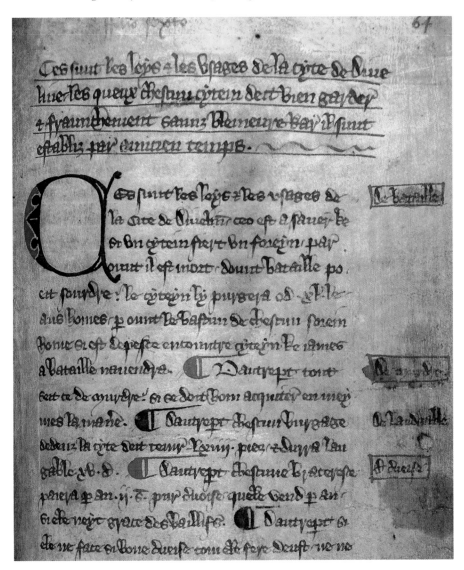

Law and Usages of City of Dublin, c. 1315. (DCLA, Chain Book of Dublin, fol. 64a)

together to demand concessions from the civic government, and these were entered by the town clerk into the White Book under the title *Grievances of the Common Folk of Dublin*. Around the same time, the *Laws and Usages of the City of Dublin* were inscribed in the Chain Book. The significance of these documents is that both texts were written, not in legal Latin, but in the spoken language of Dubliners at that time, which was Norman-French. The town clerk arranged for the decoration of the *Laws and Usages* with illuminated capital letters and colophons (or markers showing the beginning of each paragraph)

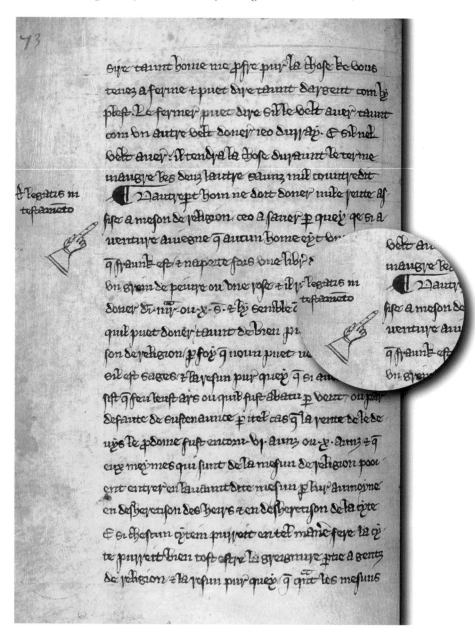

coloured in red and blue. Laws of special importance were highlighted: one which forbade Dubliners from disinheriting their children by bequeathing their property to ecclesiastics, was emphasized by a hand drawn in the margin, with a finger pointing to the law in question. The *Laws and Usages* also confirmed that the people of Dublin were to have their town clerk and that he was to be paid a salary of five marks yearly.

Law and Usages of Dublin City : Prohibition of bequests by citizens to ecclesiastics and detail. (DCLA, Chain Book of Dublin, fol. 73)

From the mid-15th century onwards, Dublin's administration became increasingly complex, and the town clerk had an augmented role in this process. Meetings of the civic government, the Dublin City Assembly, were held quarterly, at the great feasts of Easter, Midsummer, Michaelmas and Christmas and the town clerk recorded the minutes of these meetings on parchment sheets which were sewn together to form one long continuous roll. Until 1452, the minutes were written in Latin, but after that date they were written in English, which had replaced French as the spoken language of Dubliners. This may reflect an improvement in general literacy, suggesting that some members of the City Assembly were able to read, at least in English, and that they wanted the minutes in a language which they could understand. Occasionally, the minutes were accompanied by drawings in ink, illustrating decisions which were taken, or incidents which occurred, and these may have been produced for illiterate members of the City Assembly. In 1454, a ship landed a cargo of iron in Dublin and its mariners disputed the Mayor's right to levy custom duties on the freight. This controversy is described in the assembly roll and is illustrated by a drawing of the ship in question. The citizens of Dublin were also expected to provide themselves with arms, including a longbow and sword, to defend the city from attack, and here a sketch depicts an armoured man ready for battle. Apart from compiling the assembly rolls, the town clerk produced a franchise roll, which recorded the names of the free citizens of Dublin and this has survived for the period 1468-1512. Each paragraph began with the words "Memorandum

Top: Drawing of ship which delivered iron to Dublin, 1456. (DCLA, Assembly Roll 1, membrane 8b).

Middle: Drawing of Dublin Citizen ready for battle, 1454. (DCLA, Assembly Roll 1, membrane 7).

Left: Ornamental letters M for Memorandum, 1477. (DCLA, Fr/Roll/2, membrane 9/46).

Left: Ornamental letters M for Memorandum, 1477. (DCLA, Fr/Roll/2, membrane 10/1).

Below left: Dublin City Treasurer's accounts, 1539. detail showing grotesque head. (DCLA, MR/35, fol. 5a).

Below right: Signature of Town Clerk, John Dillon, 28 November 1563.(DCLA, White Book of Dublin, fol. 118b).

quod" – "Be it remembered that" and to relieve the tedium of writing these over and over again, the town clerk amused himself by devising variations for the capital letter "M" for "memorandum".

The Reformation brought many changes to Dublin. At the Dissolution of the Monasteries, the city received the lands of the Priory of All Hallows from Henry VIII and this meant a vast increase in its estates, which now included lands in the counties of Dublin, Meath, Kildare, Louth, Tipperary, Kilkenny and elsewhere. Since much of the city's revenue came from letting out its property, this in turn generated an increased income. From 1540 onwards, the City Treasurer began to maintain regular accounts which were audited each year in November; in a break with the earlier tradition of record-keeping in the city, these accounts were written on paper, instead of parchment. Again, the clerk whiled away the monotony of preparing these entries by ornamenting capital letters with grotesque heads and faces. In 1560, the Treasurer agreed to pay a

twice-yearly fee to town clerk John Dillon "...in consideration of his pains taken, and to be taken [concerning] the treasury book of this city, and in writing of bills of cess and other writings for the city's affairs". This arrangement was formally confirmed when Dillon's successor George Russell was appointed in 1577 and it was agreed that he should receive three pounds Irish for his work on the city accounts, in addition to his regular annual salary as town clerk, of forty shillings Irish. Russell lobbied to add to the duties of his office: six months after his appointment, he confirmed his right to enrol apprentices in the trade guilds of Dublin and to issue them with their indentures at a fee of 4d for each enrolment and 2s Irish for each indenture. He was less successful in securing a monopoly of writing bills or petitions presented to the City Assembly, but it was agreed that anyone who wished to present a bill not written by the town clerk should pay him a fee of 4d. Having built up his practice with great effort, Russell was allowed to take on an assistant in 1580 who was given responsibility for working on the city accounts.

Pre-occupied with the status of his office, Russell seems to have neglected the physical safety and storage of the documents in his care, and after his death in 1595, it was discovered that "several of the records of the city are erased and defaced by reason no covering is had for them". Alarmed, the City Assembly appointed a professional clerk, William Gough, to succeed Russell, and instructed him to "make up the records in a uniform manner" and to provide "a covering for the same". For greater security, the records were to be "kept under lock" so that no-one would have access to them except "such as have charge thereof". Gough was elected as an alderman in 1596 and was sent to London in the following year to present a claim for compensation to the court of Elizabeth I, after a cargo of gunpowder exploded while it was being unloaded at the Dublin quays, with great loss of life and damage to property. This left him with little time to discharge his duties as town clerk, and there is some evidence to suggest that he appointed a deputy in his place. Elected as Mayor of Dublin in 1603, Gough contracted the plague during his term of office and died in 1604. Inevitably, his part-time tenure of his post meant that the city records were still not fully secure and after his successor John Malone took office it was found that "sundry rolls and ancient muniments or records were dispersed into sundry hands". A committee was set up to investigate the matter, with powers to prosecute anyone who refused to restore the records voluntarily, but the situation was unresolved when Malone died in 1607.

Malone was succeeded by Thady Duffe, a professional clerk who was a member of a landed Dublin family with long-standing connections to the civic administration. Duffe worked hard to secure the return of "divers charters, books, rolls and muniments belonging to the city [which] had come into the hands of certain citizens by sinister means". The task was made especially difficult, as it was suspected that some documents had been taken abroad, but all recovered materials were placed safely in the Treasury House within the Tholsel. Duffe's tenure was long and successful and he was renowned for his "learned counsel". In addition to his existing duties, Duffe was responsible for licensing carmen (who drove horse-drawn carts available for hire) and for preparing freedom beseeches and issuing freedom certificates. Although he served as City Sheriff in 1613-14 and as Mayor of Dublin in 1623-4, Duffe was careful to appoint deputies to discharge the duties of town clerk in his absence. A staunch supporter of the Stuart dynasty, he was knighted in 1623 during his mayoralty but was singled out for retribution when the Cromwellians took control of Dublin in 1647 and was dismissed as town clerk in 1649. Duffe's successor, Raphael Hunt, was a political appointment. A merchant by profession, he lacked formal training as a clerk and introduced few improvements to the office.

The restoration of Charles II took place in 1660 and the new administration in Dublin Castle was anxious to replace known Cromwellians with their own supporters. After Hunt's death in 1665, the Lord Deputy, the Earl of Ossory, wrote to the Dublin City Assembly recommending the appointment of Sir William Davys as town clerk in addition to the post of recorder, which he had held since 1661. The Assembly agreed, on condition that the two offices be separated again at the end of Davys' tenure, because they felt it was too onerous for one individual. Despite their misgivings, Davys was a success in both posts. It was due to his intervention that the title of Lord Mayor of Dublin, which had been granted in 1641 but not implemented, was conferred on Sir Daniel Bellingham in 1665. In 1667, when members of the Assembly complained that the city records were disordered, Davys arranged for copies to be entered into a volume which is known to this day as the Recorder's Book. This is preserved in the Dublin City Archives and demonstrates the arrangement of the city records, which were packed at that time into six large chests, most of which contained around forty documents. Davys' success provoked resentment and in 1672 the Lord Mayor Sir John Tottie dismissed him as recorder and town clerk, a decision which was reversed by Dublin Castle, but some months later, Davys resigned as town clerk, devoting himself to his duties as recorder until his appointment as Lord Chief Justice of Ireland in 1680.

By this time, the medieval Tholsel was in a very poor state of repair and at Christmas 1675, the City Assembly decided to build a new Tholsel on the same site in Skinners' Row. While this work was in progress, the civic administration moved to the Four Courts, which were then situated at Christ Church Cathedral. The city records were packed into two trunks which were supplied by a smith named William Turner and these were taken out of the old Treasury Rooms and put into the Four Courts. Meanwhile, a record room was planned for the new Tholsel. Thomas Graves supplied 250 deal boards for this purpose at a cost of £13-15s sterling while widow Elizabeth Younge was paid £41-15s sterling for the workmanship and wainscotting of presses made in the record room and for timber, nails and other materials used in the work. All of these measures were carried out under the supervision of the town clerk, Philip Croft. A weekly account book which was kept by Croft's staff between 1682 and 1685 gives some idea of the way in which his office was run. Regular purchases included paper, ink, pens and quills for writing; wax for sealing documents; candles, which were bought by the pound weight, for lighting the office; and coal for heating, which was bought by the ton. Parchment was rarely used; in July 1683, half a roll of parchment

THE THOLSEL

The Dublin Tholsel
From Charles Brooking's
Map of Dublin, 1728

was bought for 15 shillings. Other payments in 1683 included 1 shilling to a chimney sweep in May; 3 pence for a ruler in July; 1s 2d "to Molly for a pair of cloggs" in September; and in October £1-8s-4d to "Mark's wife" for five days' weeding in the Tholsel garden.

The new Tholsel was completed in 1685 and in that same year, James II succeeded his brother Charles II as king. James was a Roman Catholic and was anxious to place his supporters in key positions throughout his dominions. In 1687, he therefore issued a charter to Dublin which completely re-organized the City Assembly, with a new Lord Mayor, Sheriffs, aldermen and councillors and of course a new town clerk, John Kearney, a Catholic who was loyal to James. The Catholic king's reign was short-lived and after his defeat at the Boyne in 1690, the previous civic administration was restored to Dublin, together with the former town clerk, Philip Croft, whose successor Thomas Twigge, had served as a captain in the army of William of Orange.

During the 18th century, the office of town clerk was dominated by a father-and-son team, Thomas and Henry Gonne. Thomas Gonne was apprenticed to town clerk Jacob Peppard and succeeded him on his death in 1724. Gonne had to pay Dublin Corporation an annual rent of £100 for the office of town clerk, and was expected to make his living by charging fees to the public for his services. In 1734, Gonne complained that he was impoverished because of a great decay of business in his office and he had to apply for a rent rebate. He resigned in 1739, as he suffered from gout, and was replaced by his son Henry, who had served an apprenticeship to his father and was also an attorney in the court of exchequer; with his appointment, a tradition was established that town clerks had to be trained in the law and this persisted until 1893. Like his father, Henry Gonne was obliged to pay an annual rent of £100 for his office and he too found it difficult to make a living. As clerk of the peace, which formed part of his duties as town clerk, Henry Gonne was obliged to prepare indictments against criminals and other offenders. He was entitled to a fee of 13s 4d for each one but complained that "because of the poverty of the persons so tried, he does not receive his fees from one in ten". He also had difficulty in collecting a fee of 7s 6d which was due for each charity petition prepared by him for submission to the City Assembly. In spite of these difficulties, Dublin Corporation showed its support for the town clerk by building a new headquarters for him. Located in Ram Alley near the Tholsel, these offices were designed by architect John Smith (who also designed St. Catherine's Church in Thomas Street) and were constructed by the builder, John Wilson, between 1763 and 1767. When Henry Gonne retired in 1770, he delivered a large parchment book to the Corporation, containing a list of all charters, assembly rolls, title deeds and city leases in his possession; this is in the Dublin City Archives and is still consulted to determine title to civic property. In return, the City Assembly showed its appreciation of Gonne by passing a resolution of thanks, which was published in the *Dublin Journal*, *Freeman's Journal* and in *Saunders' News-Letter*. Gonne was replaced by two town clerks, who were still required to pay £100 rental, but by the end of the 18th century, the office finally began to show a profit. In 1783, the Pipe Water Committee agreed to pay an annual stipend of 25 guineas to the town clerks for attending its meetings; and in 1784, the town clerks began to act for the city's Law Committee and made considerable sums of money from this activity.

The Tholsel was one hundred years old in 1785. The building had never been sound and in the following year many of the city's records, including title deeds, were damaged by rain leaking through the roof. The town clerks immediately offered to give up their house in Ram Alley so that it could be fitted up for the custody of the records, with a safe to protect everything from fire. This afforded some respite, but in 1797, the Committee of City Leases was instructed to remove the city records to "a proper place of safety, until a new Tholsel shall be built." As a temporary measure, it was decided to build a records room in the new Sessions House (now Green Street Courthouse) and the noted architect Frederick Darley was asked to design it. The city records were moved there in 1798 under the supervision of the town clerks, and the accommodation was of such a high standard that, when it was inspected in 1806 by Record

Commissioners sent from England, it met with their warm approval. Meanwhile, the City Assembly had moved to the Exhibition House in South William Street, which was re-named the City Assembly House, so that for the first time in its history, the city's records were not housed in the same building as the city's administration. In practice, the town clerks were obliged to divide their time between the Sessions House and the City Assembly House and the storage and care of the records suffered. In 1830, the Corporation's finance committee visited the Sessions House to inspect the records. The committee found that "...the Charters, some Books, Papers and Rolls of Assembly were arranged in presses with a considerable degree of attention and in good preservation". Other records were, however, in an appalling state, lying "...in heaps on the floor, four or five feet high with a covering of dust many inches deep". To improve this situation, Alderman John Claudius Beresford was asked to make a complete arrangement and classification of the records and completed this work in 1832.

By 1840, Dublin Corporation was in urgent need of reform, along with other local authorities in Ireland. The Corporation's antiquated system of raising finance was not adequate to running a huge 19th century city, and too many people, including Roman Catholics, were excluded from election to the City Assembly by outdated regulations. The Municipal Corporations Reform (Ireland) Act was passed in 1840 to address these problems. This widened the civic franchise to include all householders, of whatever denomination, with property of a rateable valuation worth more than £10 yearly. The Act also confirmed the position of town clerk and defined his duties as: maintaining and printing the freeman's roll, which listed all the voters in the city; marking out the city's boundaries; and keeping the records of the small claims court, which was known as the Court of Conscience. In October 1841, the first municipal elections were held under the new franchise and the ruling oligarchy in Dublin was replaced by a more democratic City Council, containing representatives of the new business class in the city, many of whom were Catholics. This process was completed on 1 November 1841, when the patriot Daniel O'Connell was elected as Lord Mayor of Dublin. It was not long before the new City Council began to flex its muscles. Under the 1840 Act, it had the right to appoint the town clerk and other Corporation officials and in 1842, the Council began a systematic and sustained process of dismissing all staff who had been carried forward from the old Corporation and replacing them with new appointments. The distinguished City Architect, John Semple, was fired on 1 April 1842 and was replaced by the lesser talent of Hugh Byrne. The two town clerks, Robert Dickinson and George Archer, were dismissed in the following November, even though the City Council admitted publicly that both men had assisted them in every way, without displaying any political bias. The custom of appointing two town clerks was abandoned, and Archer and Dickinson were replaced by just one man, William Ford, a solicitor with a practice in Dame Street.

As the 19th century progressed, Dublin Corporation was given ever-increasing power in running the city and, as the principal official, the town clerk carried out more duties and had greater responsibilities than ever before. Under the Dublin Improvement Act

The City Hall, Dublin, c. 1867. DCLA, Dixon Slides, 2.32

of 1849, the Corporation took over the duties of the defunct Wide Streets Commission and Paving Board, and was also assigned the property which had been vested in those bodies. More staff was needed to discharge these new functions, and in 1852, the Corporation moved its headquarters from the City Assembly House to the larger Royal Exchange, which was re-named City Hall. The extra space afforded by this move allowed the city's records and archives to be moved from Green Street Courthouse to the new centre of civic administration. Dublin Fire Brigade was set up in 1862 and in 1868 the city's water-supply was dramatically increased with the opening of the Vartry Reservoir. From 1875 onwards, a series of Acts of Parliament gave the Corporation power to build housing for the working classes and, after the passage of the Open Spaces Act in 1887, the Corporation began to acquire property for conversion into public parks. Public libraries were opened at Thomas Street and Capel Street in 1884 and the Corporation extended its involvement in education with the opening of the Science and Art Schools at Kevin Street in 1887 and with the production of the *Calendar of Ancient Records of Dublin,* a transcript of the city's early documents edited by John T. Gilbert, which was first published in 1889. In 1892, the city's first elec-

tricity power station was opened by the Corporation in Fleet Street; in 1904, the city began to register motor vehicles; and the Dublin Main Drainage Scheme was completed in 1908. To cope with this increased work-load, the Corporation's staff expanded and the town clerk began, to a certain extent, to assume the duties of a chief executive.

The political upheaval which followed the 1916 Rising also had an impact on Dublin Corporation. The composition of the City Council changed, and the nationalist party, Sinn Fein, gained a majority of seats in the local elections of 1920. To demonstrate its independence from the Westminster Parliament, Sinn Fein refused to deal with the Local Government Board for Ireland, which was effectively part of the British Civil Service. When the town clerk, Henry Campbell, submitted the city's accounts to the local government auditor against the express instructions of the City Council, he was forced to resign from his post and was replaced by John J. Murphy. But the City Council itself was not immune from political controversy. Its members were opposed to the Anglo-Irish Treaty of 1921 and came into increasing conflict with the Irish Free State government. In May 1924, Dublin City Council was therefore suspended by the Minister for Local Government and was replaced by three commissioners, one of whom, P.J. Hernon, would later serve as Dublin City Manager. Dublin was without an elected local government until 1930, which provided a unique opportunity to review the administration of the city, and a Greater Dublin Commission was established for this purpose. Many of its recommendations were ignored, but one of great significance was put into effect: that Dublin should have a "Chief Executive Officer who would be styled and known as a City Manager" responsible to the elected Dublin City Council. This proposal became law under the Dublin Corporation Act of 1930, which also abolished the Urban District Councils of Pembroke and of Rathmines and Rathgar, bringing these Victorian suburbs into the city area and under the control of the Corporation. The first meeting of the newly-elected City Council for the Greater Dublin area was held on 14 October 1930 and the chair was taken by the first City Manager, Gerald J. Sherlock, who then presided over the election of Alfie Byrne as Lord Mayor of Dublin. Seven hundred years earlier, the first recorded town clerk, William FitzRobert, had been present at the election of Dublin's first Mayor, Richard Multon. Now, the city was entering a new era, with the town clerk taking on the executive functions of the City Manager and working with an expanded City Council in the service of a greater Dublin.

Biographies of the Town Clerks of Dublin

William FitzRobert (Town Clerk, c.1230-c.1263)

FitzRobert is first mentioned in 1230, when he was granted a plot of ground at the New Gate by the city of Dublin, in recognition of his good and faithful service as town clerk. He later built a house on the site. FitzRobert was known by the nickname *William-de-la-Choife* – a coif was a close-fitting cap which was worn by sergeants-at-law. In his capacity of town clerk, he witnessed many documents issued between 1230 and 1263. In 1260, he is recorded as being town clerk jointly with Ralph the Clerk; and he is last mentioned in 1263 when he had been joined by Roger the Clerk as town clerk. (*CARD*, vol. I, pp 82-5, 92-4, 98, 100-2; *Christ Church Deeds*, nos. 93, 485, 488, 491, 493, 499, 500, 504-6; *Chartularies of St. Mary's Abbey*, nos. 234, 245, 278; "St Werburgh's Deeds", no. 57)

Ralph the Clerk (Town Clerk, 1260)

Ralph is recorded as witness to a deed issued in 1260, when he is described as one of the town clerks of Dublin, together with William FitzRobert. (*Christ Church Deeds*, no. 506)

Roger the Clerk (Town Clerk, c. 1263-1270)

Roger is mentioned in 1263 as one of the town clerks of Dublin, together with William FitzRobert. He appears again as witness to a deed issued by the Prior of Holy Trinity in 1270, where he is described as town clerk. (*Christ Church Deeds*, nos 93 and 96)

William Picot (Town Clerk, late 13th century)

A grant of Buttevant's Tower was given by the Mayor and Commonalty of Dublin to William Picot, their beloved and faithful clerk, for his praiseworthy services. This grant is undated, but on internal evidence is believed to be from the late 13th century. (*CARD* vol. I, p. 95)

Robert Halys (Town Clerk, c.1370)

Robert Halys, town clerk, is mentioned as witness to a grant of property in Ship Street, issued in August 1370. (*Christ Church Deeds*, no. 711)

Hugh Possewyk (Town Clerk, c. 1400)

Hugh Possewyk is recorded as witness to several deeds issued between 1370 and 1400 but is described as town clerk only in September 1400. In 1391, he was granted lands in Donnybrook by Roger Kilmore. (*Christ Church Deeds*, nos 245, 255, 711, 767-9, 771, 781-2, 792, 795, 800, 806)

Thomas Schortals (Town Clerk, c. 1406-7)

Thomas Schortals is recorded as town clerk in deeds issued in 1406 and 1407. He was Bailiff of Dublin twelve times between 1406 and 1426 and was Mayor of Dublin twice, in 1424-5 and 1424-6. He held a tenement in the High Street and a garden at Wood Quay. In 1439, he received payment of debts due to him under the will of Robert Passavaunt. He died in 1445.

(*Christ Church Deeds*, nos. 271, 290, 820, 822-3, 828, 841-3, 851-3, 951, 971)

Peter Bartholomew (Town Clerk, c.1477-1493)

Peter Bartholomew (also known as Perce Bertilmewe) was appointed town clerk sometime before 1477. He was married to Joanna Waryng, a wealthy heiress with lands in Dalkey, Co. Dublin, and the couple's three daughters, Isabella, Anna and Janet, were admitted to the civic franchise at their father's request between 1477 and 1481. Their two sons, William and John, trained as clerks under their father's tutelage and received the civic franchise at Easter 1486 and Midsummer 1491 respectively. Bartholomew also had a woman apprentice, Janet White, who was admitted to the civic franchise at Michaelmas 1481 on completion of her training as a clerk. Anna Bartholomew was the only member of the family to survive her parents and in 1525 she gave her Dalkey estates to Christ Church Cathedral. (*CARD*, vol. I, pp 140-1, 378; *Christ Church Deeds*, nos. 381-2, 416, 1144-5)

Richard Allen (Town Clerk, 1493-1504)

Appointed as town clerk in July 1493 in succession to Peter Bartholomew, Allen was responsible to the Recorder, Sir James Eustace, who arranged for him to receive the civic franchise in the following October. Under the terms of his appointment, Allen was to have "all manner [of] wages, fees, rewardes, profites, clothes and other emoluments" belonging to the office of town clerk. At Christmas 1500, the City Assembly decided that the clerk should receive "a good, honest gown" from the Bailiffs "or else 13s 4d a year". (*CARD*, vol. I, pp 378, 386)

John Dillon (Town Clerk, 1556-1577)

Dillon was appointed as town clerk some time before Christmas 1556, when the City Assembly gave him a lease of void ground at Cock Hill and Cock Lane. At Easter 1559, the Assembly decided that Dillon and his successors as town clerk should be free from all taxes and cesses imposed by the city. In 1561, he was allowed a yearly fee by the City Treasurer "in consideration of his pains taken [concerning] the treasury book of this city, and in writing of bills of cess and other writings for the city's afffairs". Dillon served as an alderman on the City Assembly between 1566 and 1573 but retained his position as town clerk until 1577 when he was replaced by George Russell. Dillon's autograph appears on folio 118b of the White Book of Dublin. (*CARD*, vol. I pp 202, 460, 486-7; vol. II pp 15-16, 43, 86-7, 135)

George Russell (Town Clerk, 1577-1595)

Russell was appointed in 1577, with a yearly salary of 40 shillings Irish which was augmented by a further three pounds annually for perclosing the city's accounts and writing warrants appointing constables for the city wards. He also received fees for enrolling apprentices in the trade guilds of Dublin. In 1578, the City Assembly gave him a lease of a room built over the slip on the north side of the bridge of Dublin, at a yearly rent of 6s 8d. In 1580, it was agreed that Russell should have an assistant: this post was filled by John Dorning, a former City Sheriff who took responsibility for writing up the city accounts. After Russell's death in 1595, the city's records were found to be in very poor physical condition. (*CARD*, vol. II, pp 114, 118, 125, 142, 151-2, 289. For John Dorning, see *CARD*, vol. II, pp 151, 201-2, 250)

William Gough (Town Clerk, 1595-1604)

William Gough, a clerk by profession, was admitted to the civic franchise of Dublin in 1576 by special grace, which suggests that he was a newcomer to the city. He was married to Barbara, daughter of Patrick Gough, who was Mayor of Dublin in 1576, and the couple had two children, Mary and Patrick. In 1595, he became town clerk in succession to the late George Russell. By that date, Gough must have acquired considerable wealth, since the City Assembly asked him to supply "a nest of silver bowls, double gilded London touch, of the value of £20 sterling" as a surety for his good conduct while in office. The first duty assigned to Gough was to repair the damage caused to the city's records by his predecessor's neglect and it was decided that in future the records should be held under lock and key. Gough also produced a summary of the city charters for ease of reference. At Easter 1596, Gough was elected as an alderman on the City Assembly but retained his post as town clerk. After a disastrous gunpowder explosion destroyed a large area of Dublin in 1597, Gough was sent as city agent to the court of Elizabeth I in London seeking compensation, along with Alderman Francis Taylor. In the same year, he was confirmed in his possession of a lease of the town and lands of Ballinlower, which he held from the leper house of St. Stephen. In 1603, he was elected as Mayor of Dublin but was very unwilling to accept. At that time, it was customary for the Mayor to pay for hospitality from his own pocket, and Gough argued that, since he was not a businessman, he could not really afford the costs associated with the post. However, the City Assembly voted him the sum of £100 sterling to cover his costs and Gough became Mayor at Michaelmas 1603. Gough discharged his mayoral duties with zeal, and went out in public even though the plague was rampant in Dublin at the time. Inevitably, Gough contracted the plague and died in 1604. As a gesture of sympathy, the City Assembly allowed his widow to keep the remaining money from the £100 allowed to him as Mayor. (*CARD* vol. II, pp 110, 272, 275, 289, 306, 308, 357, 407-8, 410-11, 421-3, 426-7, 433; Lennon, *The Lords of Dublin*, pp 256-7)

John Malone (Town Clerk, 1604-1607)

The son of James Malone, a Dublin merchant, John Malone was admitted to the civic franchise in 1598, giving his profession as clerk; John's daughter, Janet, received the franchise in 1603. Appointed town clerk in 1604 on the death of William Gough, Malone was instructed to reside in the city so that he could attend the city court and wait on the Mayor when needed. He was also required to exercise the office in person and not by deputy. These terms suggest that the City Assembly was not happy with the way in which Malone's predecessor had discharged his duties and in 1605, a complaint was received that various "rolls and ancient muniments or records were dispersed into sundry hands". Before he had the opportunity to rectify this situation, Malone died in 1607. (*CARD* vol. II, pp 433, 452-3, 475)

Sir Thady Duffe (Town Clerk, 1607-1649)

Thady (or Thomas) Duffe was a member of a wealthy Dublin family which had a long-standing connection with Dublin Corporation. His grandfather, also called Thady Duffe, was Mayor of Dublin in 1548-9 and his uncle, Nicholas Duffe, was city treasurer in 1578-9 and Mayor in 1579-80. The family owned land in county Dublin and their seat was at Ballyfermot. Duffe's father, Richard, was a prominent Roman Catholic who held lands from St. Anne's guild, a lay confraternity which was active in the counter-reformation, but Thady seems to have conformed to the established church before 1613, when he served as city sheriff, as otherwise he could not have subscribed to the oath of supremacy which that official was obliged to take. He obtained the civic franchise in 1604, giving his profession as clerk, and was appointed town clerk in 1607 on the death of John Malone, on condition that he paid £20 Irish for the privilege. His first task was to recover the "diverse charters, books, rolls and muniments belonging to the city [which] had come into the hands of certain citizens by sinister means". The search proved to be long and difficult, as it was suspected that some documents had been taken abroad, but any items recovered were placed safely in the Treasury House within the Tholsel. While serving as city sheriff for 1613-14, Duffe's duties as town clerk were discharged first by a committee and later by his son Richard. Thady Duffe was elected as an alderman on the City Assembly in 1617, and served as Mayor of Dublin in 1623-24 (when he was knighted) and as city treasurer in 1625-26. During his mayoralty, a committee again discharged his duties as town clerk, until he resumed his post in 1624. A supporter of Charles I, Duffe suffered when the Cromwellian Colonel Michael Jones was appointed as governor of Dublin in 1647 and he was dismissed as town clerk in March 1649, on very doubtful grounds. (*CARD* vol. II, pp 430, 475, 507, 510; vol III, pp 7, 41, 49, 82-3, 153, 161-2, 165-6, 178, 254-5, 380-1, 405-6, 475-5; Lennon, *The Lords of Dublin*, p. 246)

Raphael Hunt (Town Clerk, 1649-1665)

A merchant by profession, Hunt was admitted to the civic franchise at Midsummer 1638 by fine and special grace, which suggests that he was not a native of Dublin. Elected as Sheriff for the civic year 1645-6, he chose to refuse the post and pay a fine of £40 sterling, rather than neglect his business. He was elected as Alderman some time before 1649, when he became town clerk after Thady Duffe's dismissal, and his appointment was probably political, as a reward for his support of Oliver Cromwell. He was Mayor of Dublin in 1650-51, when his duties as town clerk were taken over for the year by the noted Cromwellian Alderman Daniel Hutchinson, and by John Preston. Hunt then served as City Treasurer in 1652-3 and was returned as an inhabitant of St. Catherine's Parish in the 1659 census of Dublin. He was apparently in ill-health in 1663 (when Richard Blondevile was sworn in as deputy town clerk) and again in 1664 (when Philip Croft was sworn in as deputy) and died in 1665. Hunt's only innovation as town clerk was the introduction of a book into which copies of all the city leases were entered; and even this work was carried out by a committee. (*CARD* vol. I, p. 265; vol. III, pp 492, 503-4, 265)

Sir William Davys (Town Clerk, 1665-1672)

Son of Sir Paul Davys, who was secretary of state for Ireland and clerk of the Privy Council, William Davys was well-connected with the supporters of Charles II who took over Dublin Castle after the Restoration in 1660. At a special meeting of the Dublin City Assembly held the following November, Davys was admitted to the civic franchise by special grace and on presentation of a pair of gloves to the Mayoress. The City Assembly was convened again in January 1661, to appoint Davys as recorder of Dublin, with reservation to the Assembly of the right to appoint the town clerk. He was knighted some time before February 1665 when, after the death of Raphael Hunt, the Lord Deputy, the Earl of Ossory, wrote to the City Assembly, recommending the appointment of Sir William Davys as town clerk in addition to recorder: "forasmuch as we are informed that for the well-discharging the duties of that place it will be requisite that the person to succeed therein be a person knowing in the lawes". The Assembly concurred, on condition that the two offices be separated again at the end of Davys' tenure. Davys demonstrated his continuing influence with Dublin Castle when in 1665, he successfully urged the Lord Lieutenant, the Duke of Ormond, to implement a charter issued by Charles I in 1641 under which the title of Mayor was upgraded to Lord Mayor of Dublin. In 1667, the City Assembly complained that the charters and other records of the city were "so out of order and dispersed in many hands, that no ready recourse could be had thereunto, to the great prejudice of the city". To rectify this situation, Davys prepared a volume into which copies of documents were entered for ease of reference and for security: this was called the Recorder's Book and it is still preserved in the Dublin City Archives. Early in 1672, an attempt by Lord Mayor Sir John Tottie to remove Davys as town clerk and recorder was foiled by the Lord Lieutenant, but the following December Davys resigned as town clerk, continuing as recorder until Easter 1680, when he became Lord Chief Justice of Ireland. (*CARD*, vol. IV, pp 197, 333-5, 433; vol. V, pp 12-18, 55, 150, 190)

Sir John Tottie (Town Clerk, 1672-1677)
with Philip Croft

John Tottie received the civic franchise at Easter 1668 by fine and special grace, when he was returned as a shoemaker. He served as Sheriff of Dublin for the civic year 1657-8 and was knighted before 1671, when he was elected as Lord Mayor of Dublin. Early in 1672, while he was still Lord Mayor, Tottie attempted to remove the sitting recorder and town clerk, Sir William Davys, but this move was foiled by the Lord Lieutenant, the Earl of Essex, who considered Tottie to be "a person of as much disloyalty as any about this city". Davys resigned as town clerk in the following December, and was replaced jointly by Tottie and Philip Croft. Always a difficult personality, Tottie fell foul of the City Assembly and was dismissed as town clerk at Christmas 1677. (*CARD*, vol. V, pp 12-18, 55, 150, 151-2)

Philip Croft (Town Clerk, 1672-1687; 1690-1693)
with Sir John Tottie, 1672-77; with Peter Ormsby, 1677-79

Philip Croft, gentleman, was admitted to the civic franchise on 14 September 1664 on payment of a fine and was sworn in as deputy town clerk on 3 October 1664. After the resignation of Sir William Davys on 2 December 1672, Croft succeeded him as town clerk, together with Sir John Tottie. Croft was retained when Tottie was dismissed as town clerk at Christmas 1677 and he was then joined by Peter Ormsby in the office. Croft supervised the construction of a record room in the new Tholsel, which was built between 1676 and 1686. He made sufficient money from his work as town clerk to allow him to purchase property and he is recorded in the pipe water accounts of 1680 as the owner of two houses in Werburgh Street. Croft was suspended from office under a charter issued by James II in 1687 but was re-instated after the Battle of the Boyne in 1690 and died in 1693. (*CARD*, vol. I, p. 265; vol. V, 55, 184-5, 188, 211, 397; vol. VI, p. 35)

Peter Ormsby (Town Clerk, 1677-1679)
with Philip Croft

Peter Ormsby was admitted to the civic franchise at Michaelmas 1669, as a member of the guild of merchants. He was appointed town clerk jointly with Philip Croft when Sir John Tottie was dismissed in 1677 but is not mentioned after 1679. (*CARD*, vol. V, pp 151-2)

John Kearney (Town Clerk, 1687-1690)

John Kearney, a supporter of James II, was appointed town clerk under a charter issued by that king to Dublin in 1687. There is no evidence to show that Kearney was a professional clerk, and his appointment seems to have been motivated by political advantage. After the Battle of the Boyne in 1690, Kearney was dismissed, as one of "those Papists who had illegally succeeded in the Corporation" and Philip Croft again took up the post of town clerk. (*CARD*, vol. I, p. 75)

Thomas Twigge (Town Clerk, 1693-1702)

Thomas Twigge, gentleman, was admitted to the civic franchise at Midsummer 1687 by special grace and on payment of a fine. He served with the army of William of Orange and was promoted to the rank of captain. On the death of Philip Croft, Twigge was elected as town clerk in June 1693 at the yearly rent of £230 sterling, with William Jones as his paid assistant. At Christmas 1697, Twigge complained that he was making a loss on the office of town clerk and he was allowed a rent rebate then and again at Easter 1701. He resigned on 7 April 1702 because of ill-health. (*CARD*, vol. VI, pp 35, 74-5, 166-7, 246, 266-7)

Jacob Peppard (Town Clerk, 1702-1724)

Jacob Peppard was admitted to the civic franchise at Michaelmas 1693, when he was returned as a member of the guild of tailors. He obtained the franchise by means of the Act of Parliament for Encouraging Protestant Strangers to Settle in Ireland, suggesting that he was an immigrant. He was appointed town clerk in April 1702, after Thomas Twigge's resignation. Working with a committee set up by the City Assembly in September 1702, Peppard's first task was to arrange and put in order all leases, deeds, papers and records of the city, a task which was completed in the following April. In 1711, Francis Skiddy was appointed to assist Peppard as deputy clerk, with special responsibility for the records of the city treasury. In 1713, during a dispute concerning Sir Samuel Cooke's claim to be Lord Mayor, charters, rolls and other documents were produced as evidence, an indication that the city's records were in good order. Peppard retired as town clerk at Christmas 1724, as he had been advised to live in the country-side for the sake of his health. His protege, Francis Skiddy, did not long survive the departure of his mentor, and he was dismissed at Michaelmas 1725. (*CARD*, vol. VI, pp 263-4, 271-2, 286, 502, 530; vol. VII, pp 283-4, 313).

Thomas Gonne (Town Clerk, 1724-1739)

Thomas Gonne received the civic franchise at Midsummer 1711, when he was returned as a member of the guild of merchants. He also served an apprenticeship to Jacob Peppard in the town clerk's office and was subsequently employed there as a clerk, making him a natural choice as Peppard's successor when the latter retired through ill-health at Christmas 1724. At Easter 1725, a committee set up by the City Assembly to enquire into the state of the Tholsel recomended that presses and drawers should be provided in the Treasury and in the Tholsel Office to contain the city records, which obviously had grown in volume since the building was completed in 1685. Gonne was contracted to pay Dublin Corporation an annual rental of one hundred pounds for the office of town clerk and was expected to make his living by charging fees to the public for his services. This proved difficult to achieve and in 1734, he successfully applied for a rent rebate owing to "...a great decay of business in his office". In 1738, he complained again that he was the only town clerk "in the kingdom" paying rent for his office and he was allowed a remittance of two years' arrears. During his career, Gonne was called as an expert witness in several law cases, including an investigation into the parish watch and city scavengers in 1729 and the city's right to the Three Penny

Customs in 1730. In April 1739, he was called to testify in a case at the House of Lords in London but pleaded unfit to go owing to "a tedious and violent fit of the gout". In vain did the City Assembly intercede with the Lord Lieutenant and Gonne left for London in May. The journey seems to have worn him out, and he retired as town clerk on his return to Dublin. Gonne and his wife Mary had three sons and three daughters; his eldest child, Henry, succeeded him as town clerk. Their descendants include the Irish patriot, Maud Gonne, and her son Sean MacBride, the founder of Amnesty International and winner of the Nobel and Lenin Peace Prizes. (*CARD*, vol. VII, pp 283-4, 294, 474, 502; vol. VIII, pp 135-6, 300-1, 331-2, 336, 343-4)

Henry Gonne (Town Clerk, 1739-1770)

Henry Gonne was admitted to the civic franchise by birth, at Midsummer 1734, as the son of town clerk Thomas Gonne. He served an apprenticeship to his father and later worked as an attorney in the court of exchequer. Like his father, Henry Gonne paid £100 sterling as a yearly rental for his office and he, too, found it difficult to make a profit, and was forced to seek rent rebates. Gonne's legal training was useful in preparing evidence for the Corporation concerning the duties of the city water-bailiff and in defence of the city's right to tolls and customs. Between 1763 and 1767, a house was built near the Tholsel in Ram Alley to serve as an office for the town clerk, an indication of his importance within the civic administration. Gonne retired in 1770 on grounds of ill-health and in a unique gesture, the City Assembly passed a resolution of thanks to him, which was published in Dublin's leading newspapers. Gonne retired to his house in Abbey Street, where he lived with his wife Margaret; he died in 1785 and was buried in St. Mary's Churchyard on 20 July. (*CARD*, vol. VIII, pp 343-4; vol. IX, pp 175-6, 194, 232-3, 241, 246; vol. X, pp 11-13, 373-4; vol. XI, pp 165-6, 374-5, 413; vol. XII, pp 65-6, 98-9, 108-9, 117; St. Mary's parish register, Dublin, 1767-1800 R.C.B. Library P.277.1.3)

Benjamin Taylor (Town Clerk, 1770-1789)

with Henry Broomer, 1770-1775; John Lambert, 1780-1784; and John Allen 1784-1789
Benjamin Taylor was admitted to the civic franchise at Midsummer 1754, the son of a skinner, James Taylor, who had prospered and become a gentleman. Having qualified as an attorney, Benjamin Taylor was appointed town clerk in October 1770 with Henry Broomer, at an annual rental of £100 sterling. From 1773 onwards, the office began to show a profit, and this was helped by the allocation of an annual salary for attending meetings of the Grand Jury, Pipe Water Committee and City Law Committee. After Broomer's death in 1775, Taylor was retained as sole town clerk, but the volume of business was too great for one person and John Lambert was appointed to assist him in 1780. On Lambert's death in 1784, John Allen joined Benjamin Taylor as town clerk until the latter's resignation on 16 October 1789. (*CARD*, vol. XII, pp 98-9, 236-7, 326-7, 357, 388-9, 409-10, 423-4, 432-7, 487-91; vol. XIII, pp 123-4, 127-8, 227-2, 313, 331-3, 362-3, 417-8, 492-3, 501-2; vol. XIV, pp 26, 84-5, 135-6 336-7, 425-6).

Henry Broomer (Town Clerk, 1770-1775)

with Benjamin Taylor

Henry Broomer was appointed joint town clerk with Benjamin Taylor in October 1770. A qualified attorney, he had already worked as clerk to the Grand Jury and in the Tholsel Court, where he "prosecuted numbers of criminals to conviction". He died in 1775. (*CARD*, vol. XII, pp 85-6, 98-9, 357, 388-9).

John Lambert (Town Clerk, 1780-1784)

with Benjamin Taylor

John Lambert received the civic franchise at Christmas 1778 by special grace, as a member of the guild of merchants. He was appointed joint town clerk on 23 June 1780 and held the post until his death in 1784. (*CARD* , vol. XIII, pp 123-4, 396)

John Allen (Town Clerk, 1784-1830)

with Benjamin Taylor, 1784-1789; and Molesworth Greene, 1789-1830

John Allen received the civic franchise at Midsummer 1777 by service, as a member of the guild of butchers. He was appointed joint town clerk on 20 October 1784, on the death of John Lambert, and retained the post until his death. (*CARD*, vol. XIII, p. 396; vol. XVIII, pp 385-6)

Molesworth Greene (Town Clerk, 1789-1834)

with John Allen, 1789-1830; and George Archer, 1830-1834

Molesworth Greene was admited to the civic franchise at Michaelmas 1785, by birth and as a member of the guild of brewers. He was appointed joint town clerk at Michaelmas 1789, on the resignation of Benjamin Taylor, and held the post until his death in 1834. (*CARD*, vol. XIV, pp 135-6; vol. XIX, p. 170)

George Archer (Town Clerk, 1830-1842)

with Molesworth Greene, 1830-1834; John Long, 1834-1839; and Robert Dickinson, 1839-1842

George Archer was a member of the guild of merchants and obtained the civic franchise at Michaelmas 1804. His father, William Henry Archer, of Somerton Lodge, Co. Dublin, was city sheriff in 1797-8 and Lord Mayor of Dublin in 1811-12. George was the only child of William Henry's first marriage to widow Margaret Shaw; another son, Henry, by his second marriage to Rebecca, daughter of goldsmith Matthew West, was the inventor of a machine for perforating postage stamps, and was one of the promoters of the miniature Ffestiniog Railway in north Wales. Other relatives included Charles Palmer Archer, of Mount John, Co. Wicklow, who was Lord Mayor of Dublin in 1832-33, and the distinguished artist, Sir Martin Archer Shee. A qualified solicitor, George Archer was appointed joint town clerk on 8 January 1830, following the death of John Allen. His term of office was dominated by the projected reform of Dublin Corporation, and in April 1838, as a member of a sub-committee set up to consult on the steps to be taken in supervising the progress of the Irish Municipal Corporation Bill, Archer went to London to see the bill through the House of Lords. Dublin City Council was created under this new act and dismissed Archer in November 1842, together with Robert Dickinson. (*CARD*, vol. XVIII, pp 385-6; XIX, pp 119-120, 170, 257-8, 317-8).

John Long (Town Clerk, 1834-1839)

with George Archer

John Long received the civic franchise at Easter 1818 by birth, as a member of the guild of saddlers. Having qualified as an attorney, Long was appointed as joint City Law Agent in October 1830 before being elected as joint town clerk on 4 December 1834, replacing Molesworth Greene, lately deceased. He held the post until his death on 2 September 1839, following a "painful and protracted illness", which he had borne "with an evenness of temper peculiarly his own". (*CARD*, vol. XIX, pp 170, 383).

Robert Dickinson (Town Clerk, 1839-1842)

with George Archer

Robert Dickinson received the civic franchise by birth at Midsummer 1834, as a member of the guild of merchants. Appointed joint Law Agent on 5 January 1835 he was elected as joint town clerk on 19 September 1839 after the death of John Long. During their time as town clerks of Dublin, Dickinson and Archer were called upon in July 1841 to have a copy of the Freeman's Book prepared, compiled from the records of the Corporation. This book was to remain in the custody of the town clerks so that any freeman might refer to it. Two hundred copies were printed and distributed among Corporation members, the expense being sustained by that organisation. From the time that Dickinson entered the Corporation, he steadfastly upheld the idea of levying a borough rate as the only means of retrieving and ultimately saving the City Assembly from danger of dissolution. Rates were introduced under the Municipal Corporations Reform (Ireland) Act of 1840, but this was not enough to save the Assembly, which was abolished and replaced by the Dublin City Council, elected on a more democratic franchise in October 1841. Under the new legislation, the City Council had the authority to appoint the town clerk, and to facilitate their own nominee, Dickinson and Archer were dismissed in November 1842, certain councillors requiring to know if they had satisfactorily delivered and accounted for all the documents that had come into their possession during their joint period in office. Most members acknowledged, however, that both men had assisted the Council in every way possible and had been free from political bias in their treatment of their various duties towards councillors and the general public. (*CARD*, vol. XIX, pp 170, 383, 436-7)

William Ford (Town Clerk, 1842-1860)

Following the dismissal of Robert Dickinson and George Archer, William Ford, of 26 Arran Quay, was elected by 35 votes on the fourth count, to the office of town clerk of Dublin, on 8 November 1842. On his inauguration, he said that he hoped to prove himself worthy of such "honest and zealous" friends who had elected him, by the faithful and efficient discharge of the important trust confided in him. Ford was a solicitor with a practice in Dame Street. He was buried in Glasnevin Cemetery on 6 June 1860. (Minutes of Dublin City Council; *Freeman's Journal*)

Alexander Farquhar (Town Clerk, 1860-1864)

Alexander Farquhar of 58 Dominick Street Upper, was appointed as town clerk on 22 June 1860. On his election, he thanked members of the City Council, "of all sections" and vowed to do his duty, "to the best of [his] ability". He was Law Agent prior to his appointment as town clerk. On Farquhar's death on 25 March 1864, a proposal was put forward by members of the City Council to erect a mural tablet to him. The ability with which he had discharged his duties had gained for him the respect and admiration of every member of the house. The deep respect entertained for him was aptly shown by the presence of the Lord Mayor's state carriage at his funeral. (Minutes of Dublin City Council; *Freeman's Journal*)

William Joshua Henry (Town Clerk, 1864-1878)

W.J.Henry, son of an eminent physician, was a highly respected member of the solicitors' profession, and was well-known in connection with the Liberal Party in Dublin during his lifetime. He was secretary of the Liberal Registration Association and earned many staunch friendships during this time, by his courtesy and geniality. He held the office of sub-sheriff previous to his appointment as town clerk of Dublin on 17 May 1864. During his time as town clerk, reference was made to the generosity of his nature and the marked ability he displayed in service of the City Council. W.J. Henry died on 14 August 1878 while on vacation in Galway. His death came after a short illness and subsequent declining health. Tributes were paid by the Council to Henry's long time in public service and to his widespread social popularity. (Minutes of Dublin City Council; *Freeman's Journal*)

John Beveridge (Town Clerk, 1878-1893)

John Beveridge entered the Civil Service in 1864, and was auditor of the Civil Service Literary Society in 1867, where he attracted the praises of John Stuart Mill. He was originally intended for the law profession, having been admitted to the Bar in 1874. Previous to this, he had entered the Civil Service, on passing a "brilliant examination", and was appointed to the Registrar-General's Office where he speedily obtained promotion to the Inspectorship of Registration, a post he held until the abolition of that office in 1876.

Beveridge was elected the following year by Dublin City Council to as secretary of the No. 1 Committee, and was well respected in this post for his great efficiency and tact. Three years later at a meeting of the City Council on 9 September 1878, Beveridge was unanimously elected to the more important post of town clerk of Dublin, which fell vacant by the death of W.J. Henry. It was said the first, Beveridge applied himself to his work, "with a zeal and devotion which it would be impossible to excel". From the beginning, he thoroughly acquainted himself with the working of all the Corporation departments, which was emphasised in his invaluable help to Corporation officers during his time as town clerk.

Beveridge took a prominent part in the leading improvements being carried out in the city at the time. He examined the Corporation debt, and was responsible for great savings in the city finances. He also gave time to the Statistical Society and was for several years a member of that council. In addition, he communicated several valuable papers on municipal and other statistical matters to its records. His main achievement as town clerk was to ensure the safe passage of the Dublin Corporation Act 1890, which strengthened the municipality's position regarding the provision of public housing. A year before his untimely death, the Corporation granted Beveridge an increase in salary, in recognition of his great value to the city. When he had to resign his post in early March 1893 due to continued ill-health, the Corporation granted him the highest retiring pension which was in their power to allow. He died on 30 June 1893 when he was only forty-eight years of age.

John Beveridge was regarded as an amiable, frank, generous man throughout his career with Dublin Corporation, and despite being a strict adherent of accuracy in all areas of work, was most considerate to those working under him. He married twice during his lifetime – to Miss Teeling, daughter of the late John Francis Teeling, Master in Chancery and to Mrs. Blackhall, widow of Nicholas Blackhall, Barrister-at-Law. His descendant, Sir Gordon Beveridge, served as vice-chancellor of The Queen's University, Belfast. (Minutes of Dublin City Council; *Freeman's Journal*)

Sir Henry Campbell (Town Clerk, 1893-1920)

Henry Campbell was appointed as town clerk of Dublin on 24 May 1893 after defeating seven other candidates for the position. Campbell had been private secretary to Charles Stewart Parnell and had supported him during "The Split" arising from the controversy over the divorce of Mrs. Kitty O'Shea, when Parnell had been named as co-respondent. A native of Kilcoo, Co. Down, where he was born in 1856, Campbell had served as M.P. for South Fermanagh in both 1885 and 1886-92 as a member of the Home Rule Party.

Sir Henry Campbell, Town Clerk of Dublin, 1893-1920

On his appointment as town clerk, Campbell stated that he would leave no stone unturned to become a "capable and efficient servant in as short a time as possible". Five months into his new post, he submitted a report to Dublin City Council on the staff employed in his office. Since taking over as town clerk, there had been an increase in the number of meetings of the Council and of Special Committees, making it necessary to employ extra help. In

September 1899, he requested the Local Government Board of Ireland to increase his salary to take account of his additional duties which were the result of greater municipal enterprise. He described the passage of legislation which benefitted the city, citing the example of the Water Bill of 1894 which was not passed until 1897, bringing a "considerably increased revenue to the Corporation". Campbell also emphasised his promotion of the Boundaries and Markets Bills, which had conferred borrowing powers on the Corporation to the extent of £700,000; as he remarked with no false modesty, the suggestion for this provision had originated with the town clerk himself. In March 1907, Campbell asked for a further increase in salary, in consequence of more duties imposed upon him by the passage of the Dublin Corporation Act of 1900, which had added a large area to the city.

In August 1912, Campbell was appointed temporarily, but this time without salary, to act as secretary of the County Borough of Dublin Insurance Committee, and was thanked for his "admirable and gratuitous work" for this committee. In April 1913, he submitted a letter to the City Council, outlining that for the past thirty years, the Corporation had done "magnificent" work and had "rendered lasting and beneficial services to the citizens" of Dublin. Since the passage of the Public Health Act of 1878, the Corporation had provided among other things, an abattoir, market, baths, disinfecting chambers, main drainage, electric lighting, technical schools, five public libraries, a sanatorium, open spaces, and several housing schemes. In recent times, the Corporation had undertaken the building of a new storage reservoir at Stillorgan, which would provide an adequate supply to the townships and the city. In looking back over his time as town clerk, Campbell noted that the income from the City Estate had greatly increased, which had enabled the Corporation to issue grants to city hospitals and other institutions for the benefit of the poor.

In the local elections of 1920, for the first time Dublin City Council had a Sinn Fein majority of 42 seats out of 80. This dismayed Campbell, who did not share Sinn Fein's aspiration for independence but instead favoured a measure of Home Rule and retaining the link with Britain. Campbell insisted upon submitting the Corporation accounts to local government auditors, against the express instructions of Dublin City Council, which refused to deal with any agency of the British Government. In December 1920, Henry Campbell was forced to resign, and Michael J. Walsh was appointed to act as town clerk *pro tem* until a permanent appointment was made.

Campbell retired to live at Greenwood Park in Newry, Co. Down, with his second wife Alice Harbottle, a widow originally from Newcastle-upon-Tyne who was the daughter of Robert Fogan. His first wife Jenny Brewis, who died in 1906, also came from Newcastle-upon-Tyne. Campbell was flamboyant in appearance, with a magnificent waxed handlebar moustache. He is mentioned in the 'Eumaeus' chapter of James Joyce's *Ulysses*, where a jarvey is described as resembling the town clerk Henry Campbell. Campbell was knighted in 1921 and died on 5 March 1924. (Minutes of Dublin City Council; *Freeman's Journal*)

John J. Murphy (Town Clerk, 1921-1927)

John J. Murphy entered Dublin Corporation in June 1891 as a rental clerk in the City Treasurer's and Estates and Finance Offices. In 1901, he was appointed as principal clerk and three years later became deputy city treasurer. He occupied this position for seventeen years and during this time, he was known to all members of Dublin City Council as a "zealous and conscientious worker." He was appointed town clerk of Dublin in February 1921 and was one of the financial experts who advised the Irish delegation to the Treaty talks in 1922. As town clerk, he witnessed controversy and upheaval, when the City Council was suspended in May 1924 and was replaced by three commissioners appointed by the government of the Irish Free State.

John J. Murphy, Town Clerk of Dublin, 1921-1927

In August 1927, the Department of Industry and Commerce recommended the appointment of Murphy as first chairman of the newly-created Electricity Supply Board. With reluctance, the city commissioners decided to grant the request, while acknowledging that this would afford an opportunity to reorganise the staff of the town clerk's department. Murphy was later to serve as chairman of McBirney's, the well-known Dublin department store, and as vice-chairman of the General Insurance Company. He died in 1947. (Minutes of Dublin City Council; *Irish Times*)

The Dublin City Managers and Town Clerks, 1930-2006

Under the management system introduced by the Local Government (Dublin) Act 1930, the civic government of Dublin consists of two elements – the elected Dublin City Council and the Dublin City Manager. There is in law a clear delineation between the powers and functions of the elected City Council, known as *reserved* functions and those of the City Manager, who exercises the *executive* functions. In general, the City Council has the reserved power to make decisions on major matters of policy and principle, including the adoption of annual estimates of expenditure; the levying of rates; the borrowing of money; making or varying a development plan; adopting a scheme of letting priorities for applicants for housing accommodation; demanding expenses from any other local authority; making, amending or revoking bye-laws; bringing enactments into force within the functional area of the local authority; and nominating persons to act on committees or other public bodies. A detailed description of these reserved functions is published annually in the Dublin City Council yearbooks. The City Council also has various powers relating to the functions of the City Manager, including the right to obtain information on any business or transaction and the right to inspect the Manager's orders. These powers enable the elected members to play a significant part in overseeing and directing the affairs of Dublin. Every function which is not a reserved function is an executive function pertaining to the City Manager, including the employment and management of staff; the management of property; collection of rates and housing rents; the acceptance of tenders; and generally the day to day administration of civic affairs.

On 14 October 1930, the first meeting took place of the Dublin City Council for the Greater Dublin area, incorporating the former townships of Pembroke and of Rathmines and Rathgar. The chair was taken by Gerald J. Sherlock, who was appointed as the first Dublin City Manager and Town Clerk under the Local Government (Dublin) Act of 1930. To mark this historic event, Sherlock chose to preface the meeting with a formal statement which described the new partnership which he hoped to see develop between management and the elected representatives. "To-day there is not merely a new City Council created, but a new system of civic government is inaugurated. In facing such a complex situation difficulties will be encountered especially in the earlier stages, but the process of adjustment can be rendered comparatively smooth by the exercise on all sides of good-will and patience. A common resolve to faithfully serve our City is the guarantee that these qualities will not be lacking when needed. In solving the many problems which confront me in my new position, I confidently count upon your sympathetic assistance". The meeting proper began with the election of

Senator Alfred Byrne as Lord Mayor of Dublin, who then took the chair, relinquished by the City Manager. Sherlock's statement fairly describes the philosophy which has governed the relationship between his successors and the City Council to this day. Certainly, there have been tensions and difficulties along the way, the most serious relating to the appointment of Sherlock's successor in 1936 (*see* biographies of P.J. Hernon and J.P. Keane, *below*), but these have always been overcome.

In 2006, Dublin City Council has 52 members representing twelve local electoral areas, with the Lord Mayor as Chairperson, and a staff of approximately 6,500 in clerical/administrative, professional, technical and wage-earning grades. The City Council holds a full meeting on the first Monday of each month (excluding Bank Holidays) and this provides a forum for councillors to obtain information on the progress of administration, by way of written questions to the City Manager, submitted not later than nine clear days before the meeting. In addition, detailed reports are submitted to the City Council by management. The City Council also has six Strategic Policy Committees (SPC) which meet during the month, as follows:

SPC 1 Economic Development, Planning and European Affairs
SPC 2 Environment and Engineering
SPC 3 Transportation and Traffic
SPC 4 Housing, Social and Community Affairs
SPC 5 Arts, Culture, Leisure and Youth Affairs
SPC 6 Financial Development and General

Each Strategic Policy Committee consists of 15 members. Two thirds of the membership of each SPC is comprised of Councillors while the remaining third consists of sectoral interests made up of representatives of social partners, community and voluntary groups, business organisations and other relevant interests at local level. Reports are submitted to the SPCs by officials with regard to the implementation of policy matters devised by the City Council.

On 31 December 2001, the office of Town Clerk of Dublin was abolished, and the chief executive is now known as the Dublin City Manager. On the same date, Dublin Corporation was also abolished, and the civic government of Dublin is now known as Dublin City Council, a term which encompasses the elected representatives, under the Lord Mayor, and the civic officials, under the City Manager. As Dublin continues into the new millennium, this underlines the close co-operation between elected representatives and civic officials in providing good and proper governance for the city.

Gerald J. Sherlock (1876-1942)
Town Clerk of Dublin, 1927-1930
Dublin City Manager and Town Clerk, 1930-1936

Gerald J. Sherlock first entered Dublin Corporation in 1894 where he was assigned as junior clerk to the City Engineer's Department. In 1910, he was chief clerk in that department and shortly afterwards was appointed supervisor of waterworks. In October 1922, he was given the additional charge of the secretarial work of the waterworks department. Appointed assistant to the town clerk in June 1926, he succeeded John J. Murphy as town clerk in 1927, following the latter's appointment as first chairman of the ESB.

Under the Local Government (Dublin) Act 1930, the town clerk was also appointed as Dublin City Manager and Sherlock had the honour of being the first person to hold that post. This was a radi-

Gerald J. Sherlock (1876-1942)
Dublin City Manager and Town Clerk,
1930-1936
Portrait by Cecelia Harrison
Courtesy Dublin City Gallery: the Hugh Lane

cal constitutional change in municipal administration with the Manager in consultation with members of the city council on all important matters involving public policy. In a tribute paid to Gerald Sherlock on his retirement, reference was made to this man who had made the new managerial system "less objectionable because of his great personality". Sherlock had at all times sought the advice of the members of the city council, and even those who found fault with the 1930 Act, admitted that under his administration, the new system had "lost its sting".

Sherlock's time in public service saw vast progressive changes in Dublin including the provision of a main drainage system; two large extensions of the city's boundaries; extensive waterworks development; the substitution of electric for horse trams; the construction of new roads and bridges; the provision of libraries and a new Art Gallery. Thousands of Corporation dwellings were built and Sherlock's name was popularly associated with the Poulaphouca reservoir and the central tower of the Vartry at Roundwood, two areas in which he was an effective negotiator.

After serving forty-three years in public service, Sherlock was obliged to resign as City Manager and Town Clerk with effect from 1 October 1936, due to ill-health. At a special meeting of the City Council on 19 January 1942, the then City Manager, P.J. Hernon, voiced the deep regret of those members present at the death of Gerald J.

Sherlock who had died five days previously. His brother, Lorcan G. Sherlock, Lord Mayor of Dublin for the years 1912-15, was among those in council who paid their tributes.

Patrick J. Hernon (1889-1973)
Dublin City Manager and Town Clerk, 1937-1955
Dublin County Manager, 1942-1955

Born in Galway on 26 January 1889, Patrick J. Hernon graduated from the National University of Ireland in 1919 with a Bachelor of Commerce degree. He then won a research scholarship to the London School of Economics. Returning to Ireland in 1921, he served in a number of different posts – he was a Local Government Inspector from 1921-23; Commissioner of the Cork Poor Law Union, 1923-4; Commissioner (part-time) Dublin Poor Law Union, 1929-30; Borough Manager and Town Clerk, Dun Laoghaire Corporation, 1930-37. When the Dublin City Council was suspended from 1924 to 1930, he had the honour of being appointed one of three Commissioners to take charge of the affairs of Dublin.

Patrick J. Hernon (1889-1973)
Dublin City Manager and Town Clerk,
1937-1955

Hernon's appointment as Dublin City Manager was controversial. Following the retirement of the first City Manager, Gerald J. Sherlock, in 1936, Dublin City Council believed that it had the right to appoint his successor, under the terms of the Local Government Act, 1930, subject to the approval of the Minister for Local Government, and they proposed J.P. Keane for the post. The Local Appointments Commission however, nominated Hernon as Dublin City Manager and Sherlock's successor. Under Section 4 (7) (a) of the County Management Act of 1940, Hernon was appointed as Dublin County Manager, a post which he held concurrently with that of City Manager. In 1943, he received an honorary Doctorate of Laws from the National University of Ireland.

Hernon was asked to reconsider his resignation upon reaching retirement age on 5 July 1955. In declining, he alluded to his thirty-one years spent as Commissioner, Borough Manager and City and County Manager. In his farewell speech, Hernon noted the many developments in local administration which had taken place during his time in public office. Progressive changes in the city included the necessity of extending the City boundary due to the building of thousands of houses and flat dwellings; improvements in water supplies; road construction; public lighting and fire fighting; and the newly improved social, health and hospital services. Hernon's name was closely associated with the slum clearance of the thirties, housing development and the Liffey Reservoir and North Dublin Drainage Scheme. The City Council made particular reference to the manner in which Hernon had implemented the County Management Acts, and the smooth functioning of the Corporation and Council under these Acts.

To date, P.J. Hernon has been the longest-serving City Manager and Town Clerk of Dublin, with a lengthy eighteen years in service at the head of what may be termed the largest business in Ireland. He died in August 1973.

John P. Keane (1890-1979)
Acting City Manager and Town Clerk, 1936-1937
Dublin City Manager and Town Clerk, 1955-1958
Dublin County Manager, 1955-1958

Born in 1890 in Swords, Co. Dublin, John P. Keane was a pupil of the O'Connell Schools in North Richmond Street. He obtained first place in an examination for Dublin Corporation clerkships in February 1909 and shortly afterwards, was appointed to the City Accountant's Department, where he remained until July 1922. He was then appointed staff officer in the Finance and General Purposes Department, where he was co-ordinator of all staff matters.

On the appointment of the City Commissioners in 1924, following the dissolution of Dublin City Council, Keane was entrusted with the entire secretarial work of the finance section, dealing with all matters of Corporation finance, including the salaries and wages of

John P. Keane (1890-1979)
Dublin City Manager and Town Clerk,
1955-1958

employees, conditions of service and pensions. For the first Civic Week, held in 1927, he had charge of the booking and stewarding arrangements for all civic functions, and due to his efficient management, the event was a great success. In 1929, Keane was unanimously elected as president of the Irish Local Government Officials' Union, a lasting tribute to his popularity and efficiency as a Dublin Corporation official. Up to this point, he had been in touch with the most important branches of the city's finances for a period of twenty years.

On Gerald J. Sherlock's retirement in 1936, Keane was appointed acting City Manager and Town Clerk of Dublin, the first appointment of its kind, pending a permanent appointment. Keane had been the officer responsible for advising Sherlock on staff matters in the Corporation and was financial advisor to the City Manager and the City Council. On taking up the post of acting City Manager, he foresaw the need for the building of more houses for the working classes and the advancement of the Poulaphouca Waterworks Scheme. Keane was particularly interested in the Corporation housing schemes and wanted at all costs to move people out of unsanitary conditions into a clean, healthy environment.

A dispute arose in May 1937 between the Corporation and the Local Appointments Commission. The latter had set up a board to appoint a new City Manager and had approved the appointment of P.J. Hernon. However, members of the City Council recommended the appointment of Keane, his striking ability as an administrator and the efficient manner in which he had conducted the affairs as acting City Manager, being referred to by many members of the Council. The episode dragged on for four months, after which time, Hernon was eventually appointed to the managership. Following the impasse, Keane returned in November 1937 to his former position as chief officer in charge of the Finance Department.

Keane took over the duties of T.C. O'Mahony as Assistant City and County Manager when the latter was appointed Director of Housing in 1948. Keane had at this time, charge of Dun Laoghaire Corporation, Grangegorman Mental Hospital Board, Balbriggan Town Commissioners and Deansgrange Burial Board. Under his new appointment as Director of Health, he still retained charge of the Grangegorman Mental Hospital Board.

In July 1950, Keane was one of eleven people appointed by the Ministers for Finance and Agriculture to be a member of the Racing Board. In December of that year, he was also one of the directors of the radiography service. In 1957, Keane, (a keen race goer himself, according to newspaper reports!), was appointed as director of the Racing Board. He thought that Irish bloodstock should receive more publicity in the United States, and was involved in securing Joe Hirsch, a leading American racing journalist with the American "Morning Telegraph", to come to Ireland to deliver a series of lectures on racing. Keane was appointed to the National Stud Committee in March 1957.

In the same month, Keane and his wife accompanied the Lord Mayor, Robert Briscoe for a three week visit to the United States and Canada. This trip was a move on the Lord Mayor's part to attract American industrialists to Ireland. While there, Keane met up with Oliver St. John Gogarty, with whom he had come into contact some forty years earlier – Gogarty had in fact operated on Keane's sinuses! Keane wittily concluded that he hoped Gogarty's technique had quickly improved thereafter! During the American visit, Keane was applauded for his dry wit and his oratorical skills. He made a special visit to Westfield, situated on Lake Erie in New York State, in order to get some ideas for the construction of a new city hall in Dublin. He was especially interested in the Williamsburg architecture of Westfield's city hall, and was briefed on the mayor-council form of government there. He noted that in the United States, the mayor, usually an executive officer, carried on similar duties to those of the Dublin City Manager.

J.P. Keane retired just six months short of half a century as an administrative official of the city of Dublin. In looking back over his years in the post of City and County Manager, he noted that from 1922, the Corporation had raised £54m through joint stock issues and mortgage loans. The most important development however during his time in the Corporation had been in relation to housing. In addition, the Corporation's association with the ESB in the finalising of the hydro-electric scheme at Poulaphouca further enhanced the city's municipal water supply. The city's five public libraries had increased threefold, as had the expenditure on the health services which now amounted to £3m, half of which was defrayed by the State. In Keane's forty nine years with Dublin Corporation, he had been "an outstanding official" and had the "highest qualities of mind and integrity". In 1950, he was a founding member and chairman for the first five years of the municipal mass radiography association, and a member of the committee of the National Association for Rehabilitation. He relinquished office as City and County Manager on 18 October 1958 and T. C. O'Mahony took up the post.

Keane carried on an active life well into retirement – he was director of the National Stud at Tully, Co. Kildare and chairman of the Irish Racing Board in 1962. He was also president of the Civics Institute of Ireland in 1961. In 1962, Keane was one of a five-man commission set up to investigate the CIE pension scheme and sickness benefits; their first meeting was held in June 1963 in the offices of the Department of Industry and Commerce in Dublin. To complement his workload, Keane remained an enthusiastic golfer and a regular theatre-goer.

John P. Keane died on 13 January 1979 and was buried in Dean's Grange Cemetery. His son Ronan was well-known in legal circles and was appointed Chief Justice of Ireland's Supreme Court in the year 2000.

Timothy C. O'Mahony (1900-1991)
Dublin City Manager and Town Clerk, 1958-1965
Dublin County Manager, 1958-1965

A native of Castleisland, Co. Kerry, Timothy O'Mahony worked as an accountant with J.K. O'Connor & Sons, P.H. McElligott & Sons and W.H. O'Connor, Castleisland and Dublin. He also worked on a part-time basis as press correspondent with the Kerryman Newspapers from 1918 to 1926. Later in 1926, he was appointed chief clerk with H. Coleman and Co., Public Auditors, Dublin, where he remained for a year.

O'Mahony started his public career as Superintendent of the Kerry Board of Health and Public Assistance in 1927. Three years later, he was appointed Town Clerk of Dundalk and became secretary of Leitrim County Council in 1935. He was City Manager of Limerick from 1936 to 1938 when he was appointed borough manager of Dun Laoghaire. During this time, he also acted as manager of a number of hospital and local boards. He served thirty-eight years in public service, some of that time spent as housing director, to which he was appointed in 1948, where his name was popularly associated with the elimination of slums and the provision of new housing.

Timothy C. O'Mahony, Dublin City Manager and Town Clerk 1958-1965

O'Mahony was appointed Deputy City Manager in August 1955. Then, on 18 October 1958, the Local Appointments Commission recommended the appointment of Timothy O'Mahony, "Altona", 18 Alma Road, Monkstown for the joint post of City Manager and Town Clerk and County Manager. Due to ill-health, O'Mahony was forced to resign from the office of City and County Manager on 22 August 1965, a year before he was due to retire. In a tribute paid to him for his years of service, the Lord Mayor said he feared that O'Mahony's duty to the housing crisis had taken its toll on his health, in particular the Fenian Street/Bolton Street tragedies of 1963, when four people were killed following the collapse of sub-standard private housing after a severe thunderstorm. Following a request from the Minister for Local Government, O'Mahony was appointed City and County Manager temporarily until September 30, 1965 (under the City and County Management (Amendments) Act, 1955).

Since starting into public life, O'Mahony said that he had seen many revolutionary changes, and cited the local authorities as the main example. These bodies had now the power to acquire and redevelop commercial and industrial slums where formerly they had power only to deal with buildings used for habitation. He stated his belief that the co-operation of the elected representatives and the Manager was an essential element of the management system.

Timothy C. O'Mahony also acted as Commissioner of Bray Urban District Council for 1969-70. He died on 15 December 1991.

Mathew Macken (1911-1994)
Dublin City Manager and Town Clerk, 1965-1976
Dublin County Manager, 1965-1976

Born in Co. Galway in 1911, Mathew Macken graduated from UCG in 1933 with a Bachelor of Commerce degree. The following year, he was chief ledger clerk with Comhlucht Siucre Eireann Teo, Tuam, a post he retained until 1938 when he was appointed chief clerk of the Joint Mental Hospital Board in Ballinasloe. He was county secretary with Galway County Council from 1944 until 1946, after which he was appointed City Manager for Limerick.

Macken was Founder Director of the National Mass-Radiography Association from 1950-55. He also served as a member of the Special Advisory Committee on over-crowding in Mental Hospitals, 1955; National Health Council, 1958-71;

Mathew Macken, Dublin City Manager and Town Clerk, 1965-1976

Commission on Itineracy, 1960-63; and the Commission of Inquiry on Mental Illness, 1961-66. Macken was County Manager for Kildare and Carlow for six years before being appointed City and County Manager for Dublin on 1 October 1965, a post he went on to hold for eleven years. He was also Chairman of the County and City Managers' Association, 1964-66.

Under section 5 of the City and County Management (Amendments) Act, 1955, Macken was temporarily appointed City Manager and Town Clerk and County Manager from 15 April 1976, until a permanent appointment was made in July of that year. During his term of office as City and County Manager, it was necessary to provide much of the infrastructure for the development of the growth areas of Tallaght, Clondalkin/Ronanstown and Blanchardstown to the west of the city. This entailed the construction of major sewerage and water schemes and the acquisition into public ownership of large tracts of land. Macken was given a standing ovation by the City Council on his retirement in July 1976, when tributes were paid to his exertions as Manager, and it was unanimously agreed that the many projects in the city and county were a "legacy of his dedicated work".

From 1969 until 1974, Macken spent the period as City Manager without a city council, following the then Minister for Local Government, Kevin Boland's abolition of the council for not striking a rate. During that time, a City Commissioner was appointed to carry out the functions of the council.

Macken's career did not end after retiring from the Managership – he was governor of the Irish Times Trust and a director of Irish Times Ltd. from 1976. Also in 1976, he was administrative adviser to the Royal Dublin Society, a position he held until 1981. Other posts included – director of Ballsbridge Sales Ltd. (1978-85); director, Ballsbridge Tattersalls Ltd. (1979-85); director, First National Building Society (1976-86). Macken then went on to become chairman of the First National Building Society from 1979-80 and 1984-85. Mathew Macken died on 21 April 1994.

James B. Molloy (1917-1991)
Dublin City Manager and Town Clerk, 1976-1979
Dublin County Manager, 1976-1979

James Molloy joined Dublin Corporation in 1935 at the age of 18 as a junior clerk at £2 a week and worked his way up to become Class A Clerk with the Corporation from 1946-50; Minor Staff Officer, 1950-54; Senior Executive Officer, 1954-55; Assistant Principal Officer, 1955-58; Principal Officer, 1958-66. Molloy, in fact, worked his way up through all the grades to become Assistant City Manager in 1969.

Molloy was responsible for the drafting of the first development plan in 1963. In 1966, he was appointed assistant manager with overall responsibility for the borough of Dun Laoghaire and was subsequently delegated to take charge of roads.

James B. Molloy (1917-1991)
Dublin City Manager and Town Clerk,
1976-1979

He was given the added responsibility of housing co-ordinator of Dublin City and County in 1974. Molloy was a member of the Public Service Advisory Council from 1976-77. The first native of Dublin to be appointed City and County Manager, J.B. Molloy, 8 Vernon Drive, Clontarf, Dublin 3, spent forty-one years with Dublin Corporation before being assigned the above post, which he took up from 6 July 1976. As former housing co-ordinator for Dublin, Molloy's main priority upon taking on the role of City and County Manager was to encourage housing development. He said that he wanted to see more renewal in the inner city residential areas. This was already in operation but Molloy believed that inducements should also be given to private developers in an attempt to redevelop areas concerned, in particular, the city centre. He cited the example of people moving back to the Liberties over the course of 1977 to live in vastly improved conditions as a result of redevelopment.

Molloy also felt that the various local authorities in Dublin city and county would continue to exist and that there would have to be greater co-operation between them, as there were fundamentally different problems facing the city, where renewal was most needed, and the county, which needed more input of growth. His view was that there should be an increase in public representation on the county council, which he saw as playing a more important role in local government in the future, due to the county's increasing growth, which in turn would entail the provision and maintenance of more houses. Molloy went on to say that the quality and standard of elected representatives was much higher than in recent years, and he called for some form of remuneration for the work they did.

Molloy served under every city manager since the post was created in 1930. In an interview for the *Irish Times* on his retirement, he claimed to having never "switched off" from the time he started working in the Corporation forty-one years before, and listed his hobbies as reading, " ... all the best paperbacks I can get my hands on" – and golfing.

Molloy was a member of the National Executive of the Irish Wheelchair Association from 1984. A qualified accountant, his brother was the Irish Ambassador to the United States, John Molloy. James B. Molloy died on 18 July 1991.

Francis J. Feely (1931-)
Dublin City Manager and Town Clerk, 1979-1996
Dublin County Manager, 1979-1993

Born in Dublin in 1931, Frank Feely was the son of Thomas Feely, who was one of the original members of An Garda Siochana, having joined the force on its foundation in 1922. Frank Feely, a qualified accountant, was educated at the Christian Brothers School in Synge Street, which also produced the broadcasters Gay Byrne and Eamonn Andrews. He joined Dublin Corporation in 1949 as a clerical officer and was promoted to Class A officer in 1955 and organization and methods officer in 1960. Other appointments included: assistant principal officer, 1962-66; principal officer, 1966-69, and assistant City and County Manager, 1969-79.

In July 1979, Frank Feely was appointed as Dublin City Manager and Town Clerk

Francis J. Feely, Dublin City Manager and Town Clerk, 1979-1996

and Dublin County Manager. His term of office saw a revitalization of Dublin, particularly in the historic inner city. This was spearheaded by the construction of new social housing in the Liberties in the late 1970s, an innovation which was introduced by Frank Feely as Assistant City Manager. In 1984 he recommended the introduction of tax incentives to encourage the development of private housing in the inner city. These were introduced in 1986 and since then a number of incentive schemes brought private housing into the city centre, creating employment in the building industry and re-creating a living community in the historic core. Old sub-standard housing was demolished and many older housing schemes upgraded. Temple Bar and the Custom House Docks area were transformed by imaginative renewal schemes, funded in part by the European Community (now European Union) while the Liffey Quays were redeveloped. Pedestrianisation of Dublin's premier shopping streets, especially Grafton Street and Henry Street, together with the development of a number of inner city parks, made it a pleasure to shop in the city and have attracted visitors and Dubliners alike. The revitalization of the city saw a boom in tourism and Dublin is now regarded by visitors as the most popular capital in Europe. The new award-winning Civic Offices opened in 1995 are regarded as one of the finest modern buildings in Dublin. Improvements in services were also brought about, and in any one year some 90 million gallons of water are pumped into the city every day; 200,000 tons of refuse is collected from homes and swept from city streets; and some 2,500 planning applications are processed – to name but a few! The Corporation also dealt with one million motor tax and driver licence applicants yearly as well as maintaining 70,000 public lights in the city, while 4 million loans were made each year from the public libraries.

Frank Feely has always been proud to be a "Dub" and has an encyclopaedic knowledge of Dublin's songs, literature and history. He actively fostered a sense of pride in Dublin, through the Millennium celebrations of 1988, which he originated, and the European City of Culture festivities in 1991. He took particular pleasure in introducing "welcome home" and other celebrations for sporting champions and others who were honoured by the city. An accomplished artist, he is happiest at his easel on a Sunday morning, painting a portrait of the Ha'penny Bridge.

Frank Feely was the first recipient of the Lord Mayor's Awards in 1989 and of the Gold Cluster Award for services to Tourism. He was President of the Institution of Public Administration for the six years to 1992 and chairman of the City and County Managers' Association in 1994-95. He served on a number of boards notably Dublin Promotions Organisation Ltd., Dublin City Enterprise Board, Dublin Tourism and the Operational Committee of the Dublin Regional Authority.

He was well known abroad as a representative of his native city and as an advocate of investment in job creation and tourism in Dublin. On three occasions he visited the U.S. together with the Lord Mayor of the day and the then Lord Mayor of Belfast to promote peace and investment. Amongst the presentations made to him on his retirement were gifts from the Mayor of San José and Irish Organisations in San José and the Union of Capital Cities of the European Union.

The minutes of Frank Feely's final council meeting record that the Lord Mayor paid tribute to him for the enormous contribution he had made to the Corporation and to the city during his term of office as City Manager and during his previous service. He stated that the City Manager had contributed greatly to the transformation of Dublin in recent years and that he had set the highest standards which any successor would find it most difficult to emulate. He wished Mr. Feely a long and active retirement. Members representing every group on the Council joined the Lord Mayor in paying tribute to Mr. Feely. They complimented him in particular on his accessibility, his impartiality and his wide participation in the life of the city. His initiative in bringing forward the celebration of Dublin's Millennium in 1988, his contribution to the City of Culture Celebration in 1991 and his central role in the twinning with San José in 1986 were particularly praised. Members also acknowledged his role in proposing the tax incentives which had been instrumental in promoting Inner City urban renewal. The successful completion of the Civic Offices during his term of office was also referred to. Frank Feely retired as Dublin City Manager on 13th May 1996. He now acts in a voluntary capacity as Deputy-Chairman of Our Lady's Hospital for Sick Children, Crumlin.

John Fitzgerald (1947-)
Dublin City Manager and Town Clerk, 1996-2001
Dublin City Manager, 2002-2006

John Fitzgerald was born in Galbally, County Limerick in 1947. He qualified as an accountant while working in industry and then moved to Cork Corporation as City Finance Officer. He subsequently took up duty as Dublin City Treasurer before moving to the position of Dublin Assistant City and County Manager. Under the reorganisation of local government in Dublin, John Fitzgerald was involved in the formation of the new county councils of Dún Laoghaire-Rathdown, Fingal and South Dublin and was appointed first County Manager for South Dublin in January 1994. He was appointed Dublin City Manager and Town Clerk in June 1996. That title changed to Dublin City Manager under the provisions of the Local Government Act 2001 with effect from the 1st January, 2002. His original appointment was for a

John Fitzgerald, Dublin City Manager and Town Clerk, 1996-2001
Dublin City Manager. 2002-2006

term of seven years but this was extended in 2003 for a further three years. (Ten years is the maximum period that a City or County Manager can serve under the provisions of the Local Government Act 2001.)

Above: The regeneration of Ballymun (Photograph Eamonn Elliott)
Following page: Statue of James Larkin with the Spire in the background (Photograph Barry Mason)

Shortly after his appointment John Fitzgerald initiated a programme of consultation with the people of Dublin to identify their expectations and needs from the then titled "Dublin Corporation". He also undertook a critical review of the structures within and the services delivered by the Corporation. New structures were put in place – six Strategic Policy Committees were established, along with a Corporate Policy Group and five Area Committees. Nine Regional Offices were also established. Civic Centres in Ballymun, Ballyfermot and Darndale provided a form of "one-stop shop" where people could walk in and obtain information on a range of services available to them from Dublin City Council, while providing a contact point for residents, community groups and the local business community.

Under John Fitzgerald's leadership Dublin was transformed into a world-class city. Dublin is currently Europe's fastest growing city fuelled by a booming economy, and although this dynamic created a challenge, it also offered an opportunity to ensure that change was managed in a responsible but innovative manner. The city is now ranked as one of the top destinations in Europe. With a thriving economy Dublin has attracted and embraced an emerging multi-cultural identity.

Many demands and challenges were faced by Dublin City Council during this time. Whole areas of the city have been or are in the process of being transformed and the regeneration programmes have culminated in the development of new retail and commercial centres, alongside residential development. The regeneration of Ballymun is

Above: Pearse House. Below: The Boyne Street reconstruction (Photographs Alastair Smeaton)

due to be completed within the next few years which will result in a new town the size of Sligo but only three miles from Dublin. An integrated area planning approach has resulted in a welcome return to city living, with 105,000 residents now living in the city centre, a population increase of 37% since 1991. Investment in the city centre is buoyant and City Council framework plans are on target to promote further commercial development and to create more good quality, high density housing in the city.

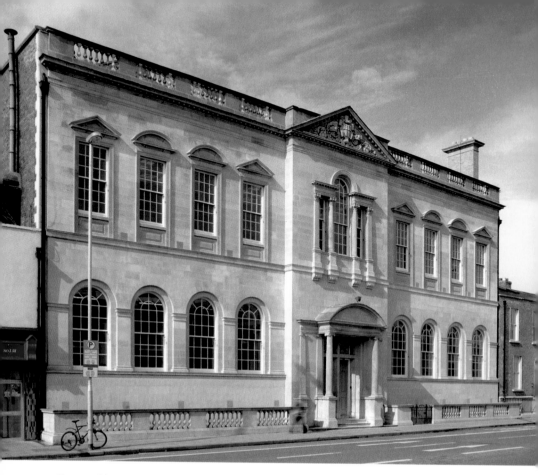

Above: Dublin City Library and Archive, Pearse Street (Photograph Barry Mason)
Opposite top: City Hall (Photograph Davison & Associates)
Opposite bottom: Dublin City Gallery: the Hugh Lane (Photograph Paul Heffernan)

Among the major projects completed during John Fitzgerald's term of office were: the O'Connell Street Rejuvenation Project which included the construction of The Spire; the Liffey Boardwalk, which provides a unique pedestrian route cantilevered over the river from Grattan Bridge to Butt Bridge; and the Dublin Bay Project which consists of a new pumping station at Sutton and a submarine pipeline across the bay to bring wastewater to a new Treatment Plant at Ringsend. The Treatment Plant opened in June 2003 and within a few years has dramatically improved the water quality in the bay and also enabled Dollymount Strand to qualify for Blue Flag status. Other major Housing/ Engineering/Waste Management Projects were put in place such as the North Fringe Sewer, Water Conservation Project, and the Quality Bus Corridor Network, which have had a huge impact on the living conditions of people in Dublin. The physical and social environment of the City Council's housing stock has also been renewed beyond all expectations and recent examples include the refurbishment of Pearse House, an Art Deco flat complex dating from the 1930s, and the reconstruction of housing at Boyne Street to create duplexes over apartments at ground level, with courtyard gardens and flowerbeds raised to a height suitable for people in wheelchairs to engage in gardening. Cultural projects included the restoration of Dublin's City Hall, one of Ireland's finest

neo-classical buildings, which was triumphantly returned to its original Georgian configuration as a millennium project; the refurbishment of Dublin City Library and Archive, which provides spacious research, exhibition and conference facilities; and a major expansion of Dublin City Gallery: The Hugh Lane, with the construction of a contemporary wing boasting thirteen new galleries to complement the existing gal-

Above: Red Stables Studios. Below: The Lab (Photographs Michael Durand)

leries in Charlemont House. In June 2005, the Red Stables Studios opened at St. Anne's Park, Raheny, to provide support for professional artists and craftworkers who wish to take new directions and set challenges for themselves and their audiences. Also in 2005, The Lab opened in Foley Street as a centre for Dublin's dynamic City Arts Office and has already become a popular venue for exhibitions, discussions and theatre, as well as the headquarters for the very successful annual Dublin Writers' Festival.

Above: LUAS on St. Stephen's Green. (Photograph RPA) Below: The Millenium Bridge

Transportation links were improved with the introduction of the LUAS light-rail system and by the construction of two new bridges over the Liffey: the pedestrian Millennium Bridge and James Joyce Bridge while the historic Ha'penny Bridge was carefully restored. 2006 will see the opening of the Dublin Port Tunnel at an estimated cost of 752 million euro. It is intended to remove most of the heavy goods vehicles

The James Joyce Bridge by architect Santiago Calatrava (Photograph John Jordan)

from the city streets. The Port Tunnel is ranked among the largest urban road projects currently being implemented in Europe. The regeneration of Parnell Square has also begun and other projects to follow include the construction of a new Liffey bridge at Macken Street which will be called after the writer Samuel Beckett.

John Fitzgerald was chairperson of the steering group which prepared and monitors the Strategic Planning Guidelines for the Greater Dublin Area. He contributed to the work of a number of agencies involved in the promotion of local government in the Dublin region and nationally. In November 2004, John was conferred with an honorary Doctorate of Philosophy by the Dublin Institute of Technology in recognition of his outstanding contribution to the development of Dublin City.

Undoubtedly, John Fitzgerald has been an enormously important force in the improvement and modernisation of Dublin City. As the last in a long line of Town Clerks of Dublin stretching back to the year 1230, and as the first Dublin City Manager of the new millennium, he has built on the best from the city's past while positioning it strategically for the future.

Appendix I:
Oath taken by the Clerk of the Tholsel
(Town Clerk), early 18th century

"You shall from hence forth beare Faithfull & true Allegiance to the Queen's most Excellent Ma[jes]tie her heirs & Lawfull Successors, you shall justly & truely enter all plaints & actions both p[er]sonall Reall & mixt between parties all Continuance & Discontinuance of writts, process or Issues you shall well & truely enter. All Declarations, Pleadings, Issues, Verdicts, and Judgments you shall likewise enter truely & justly, Also you shall true & good entry make of all Recognizances Bayles or Mainprise taken before the Mayor, Recorder and Sheriffes or any of them, All appeals, Indictments and Pleas of the Crowne you shall likewise Faithfully enter, All amerciaments & Fines offr'd & Entreated by the Court you shall truely enter the same, all orders of Assemblys according to the Indorsments of the Bills preferr'd to, and pass'd by the Assembly you shall truely enrole – true Certificate of all the Records of the Court upon writs of Certiorar you shall faithfully make to any Superiour Court and true Causes Certifie upon all writts of Corpus Cum Causa or habeas Corpus unto the Superiour Courts with the true Certificate or removement or all Records out of this Court by writs of Error out of the Superiour Courts, or by writs of false Judgment from any of the said Courts, All warr[an]ts. of Attorny., Imperlances Peremptory days and days of Grace given to any in this Court you shall faithfully and truely enter, and all the writs process Rolls Records & Minuments [sic] of the Court of Assemblys of the City you shall faithfully and truely keep safe under Lock and Key, These and all other things that the Clerk of the Tholsel ought to do, you shall for your part to the uttermost of your Power & Learning execute, observe, fulfill & keep, So help you God and by the Contents of that Book." (DCLA, Book of Oaths, MR/32)

Note: This oath was taken during the reign of Queen Anne (1702-14). It sets out the duties of the town clerk at that time, including entering the records of the city courts; writing up orders issued by the Dublin City Assembly; and keeping the rolls, records and muniments of the city under lock and key.

Appendix II:
Town Clerks of Dublin, 1230-1930

Term of office	Office-holders	Term of office	Office-holders
c.1230-c.1263	William FitzRobert	1789-1830	Molesworth Greene, with John Allen
1260	Ralph the Clerk		
c.1263-1270	Roger the Clerk	1830-1834	George Archer, with Molesworth Greene
Late 13th century	William Picot		
c.1370	Robert Halys	1834-1839	John Long, with George Archer
c.1400	Hugh Possewyk		
c.1406-7	Thomas Schortals	1839-1842	Robert Dickinson, with George Archer
c.1477-1493	Peter Bartholomew		
1493-1504	Richard Allen	1842-1860	William Ford
1556-1577	John Dillon	1860-1864	Alexander Farquhar
1577-1595	George Russell	1864-1878	William Joshua Henry
1595-1604	William Gough	1878-1893	John Beveridge
1604-1607	John Malone	1893-1920	Henry Campbell
1607-1649	Thady Duffe		John J. Murphy
1649-1665	Raphael Hunt	1927-1930	Gerald J. Sherlock
1665-1672	Sir William Davys		
1672-1677	Sir John Tottie		
1672-1693	Philip Croft		
1677-1679	Peter Ormsby		
1687-1690	John Kearney		
1693-1702	Thomas Twigge		
1702-1724	Jacob Peppard		
1724-1739	Thomas Gonne		
1739-1770	Henry Gonne		
1770-1775	Benjamin Taylor, with Henry Broomer		
1780-1784	John Lambert, with Benjamin Taylor		
1784-1789	John Allen, with Benjamin Taylor		

Appendix III:
Dublin City Managers and Town Clerks, 1930-2006

Term of office	Appointment	Office-holders
1930-1936	14 Oct 1930	Gerald J. Sherlock
1936-1937	1 Oct 1936	John P. Keane (Acting City Manager and Town Clerk)
1937-1955	1 Nov 1937	Patrick J. Hernon [1]
1955-1958	5 July 1955	John P. Keane [2]
1958-1965	18 Oct 1958	Timothy O'Mahony [3]
1965-1976	1 Oct 1965	Mathew Macken [4]
1976-1979	6 July 1976	James B. Molloy [5]
1979-1996	3 Sept 1979	Francis J. Feely [6]
1996-2001	17 June 1996	John Fitzgerald (Dublin City Manager and Town Clerk)
2002-2006		John Fitzgerald (Dublin City Manager) [7]

1. Patrick J. Hernon was also Dublin County Manager for the period 1942-1955 and was appointed on 26 August 1942
2. John P. Keane was also Dublin County Manager for the period 1955-1958, and was appointed on 5 July 1955
3. Timothy O'Mahony was also Dublin County Manager for the period 1958-1965 and was appointed on 18 October 1958
4. Mathew Macken was also Dublin County Manager for the period 1965-1976 and was appointed on 1 October 1965
5. James B. Molloy was also Dublin County Manager for the period 1976-1979 and was appointed on 6 July 1976
6. Frank Feely was also Dublin County Manager for the period 1979-1993. He relinquished that position on 31 December 1993, when Dublin County Council was replaced by three new local authorities, Fingal County Council, Dún Laoghaire-Rathdown County Council and South Dublin County Council, each with its own County Manager, with effect from 1 January 1994.
7. The post of Town Clerk of Dublin was abolished on 1 January 2002, when the Local Government Act 2001 came into force.

Sources

Manuscript Sources (Dublin City Archives):
Roll of Free Citizens of Dublin, 1234-1249
The White Book of Dublin (Liber Albus Dubliniensis), 14th to 17th centuries
The Chain Book of Dublin, 14th to 17th centuries
Dublin City Assembly Rolls, 1447-1841
Dublin City Franchise Roll, 1468-1512
Dublin City Treasurer's Account Books, 1540-1715
Dublin City Freedom Registers, 1576-1918
Recorder's Book of the City of Dublin, 1667
Weekly account book kept by Clerk of the Tholsel, 1682-1685
Book of Oaths taken by civic officials, early 18th century
Manuscript minutes of Dublin City Council, 1841-1881

Manuscript Sources (R.C.B. Library):
Christ Church Cathedral, Dublin: Registrum Novum [18th century compilation of Cathedral deeds]
St. Mary's parish, Dublin: register of baptisms, marriages and burials, 1767-1800

Published Sources:
Printed Minutes of Dublin City Council, from 1881 (in continuation)
Dublin Corporation Printed Reports, from 1869 (in continuation)
Thom's Dublin Directory, from 1844 (in continuation)
Connolly, Philomena and Martin, Geoffrey (eds.) *The Dublin Guild Merchant Roll, c.1190- 1265* (Dublin, 1992)
Gilbert, Sir John T. and Lady (eds.) *Calendar of Ancient Records of Dublin* 19 vols. (Dublin, 1889-1944) (cited as *CARD*)
Gilbert, John T. (ed.) *Chartularies of St. Mary's Abbey, Dublin*. 2 vols. (London, 1884)
Gilbert, John T. (ed.) *Historic and Municipal Documents of Ireland, 1172-1320* (London, 1870)
Institute of Public Administration. *City and County Management, 1929-1990* (Dublin, 1991)
Lennon, Colm. *The Lords of Dublin in the Age of Reformation* (Dublin, 1989) (cited as Lennon, *Lords of Dublin*)
Lennon, Colm and Murray, James (eds.) *The Dublin City Franchise Roll, 1468-1512* (Dublin, 1998)

M.J. McEnery and Raymond Refaussé (eds.) *Christ Church Deeds* (Dublin 2001)

Murphy, Sean. "The Corporation of Dublin, 1660-1760" in *Dublin Historical Record,* vol XXXVIII, no. 1 December 1984) pp 22-35

O'Neill, Marie. "Dublin Corporation in the Troubled Times, 1914-1924" in *Dublin Historical Record,* vol. XLVII, no. 1 (Spring, 1994) pp 56-70

Twiss, Henry F. "Some Ancient Deeds of the Parish of St Werburgh, Dublin" in *Proceedings of the Royal Irish Academy* vol. XXXV, section C, no. 8, 1919 (cited as "St Werburgh's Deeds")

Newspaper Sources (Dublin and Irish Collections):
The Evening Press
The Freeman's Journal
The Irish Press
The Irish Times

Newspaper Sources (Westfield, New York, United States):
The Elizabeth Daily